The Hunger Games and the Gospel

The Hunger Games and the Gospel

Bread, Circuses, and the Kingdom of God

Study Guide Edition

Julie Clawson

Patheos Press | Englewood, CO

Study Guide Edition
Published by Patheos Press
Englewood, Colorado

12 13 14 15 16 17 18 19 20 21—10 9 8 7 6 5 4 3 2 1

Cover image: "Firebird" by Christian Darmali. Used with permission.

Library of Congress Cataloging-in-Publication Data

Clawson, Julie.
   The Hunger Games and the Gospel: Bread, Circuses, and the Kingdom of
   God
   Includes bibliographical references.
   ISBN: 978-1-939221-02-5 (alk. paper)

PRINTED IN THE UNITED STATES OF AMERICA

For information, contact Patheos Press, 383 Inverness Parkway, Suite 260, Englewood CO 80112, or find us online at
http://shop.patheos.com/collections/patheos-ebooks.

For Mike
Thank you for being my companion on this journey

Table of Contents

Introduction
Let the Games Begin

Resonances of Hope

I was a latecomer to the phenomenon that is The Hunger Games trilogy. I'd heard the buzz and friends had posted the links on my Facebook wall telling me I *had* to read the books, but there always seemed to be some other book about theology or Christian living that I needed to read first. Thus it wasn't until all three books were already out and I was finishing up a busy semester in seminary that I decided to read some fiction for a break. I treated myself to the series for my mid-December birthday, and then promptly disappeared from the world for a week during the most hectic time of the year. When I emerged from my Hunger Games cocoon a week later, eyes still red and puffy from crying like a baby at the end of the third book, I dumped the books on my husband's lap and insisted he read them immediately.

I wasn't the only one who was obsessed. After Suzanne Collins' first book in the series, *The Hunger Games*, was published in September 2008, it spent over 100 consecutive weeks on the *New York Times* Bestseller list. The next two books, *Catching Fire* (2009) and *Mockingjay* (2010), quickly joined those ranks as well. Winning numerous awards, the books soon appeared in twenty-six different translations. Sparking fan sites and Twitter news feeds, fans soon even started posting handmade t-shirts and jewelry based on the books on craft sites like etsy.com. And, of course, a mega-million dollar Hollywood film adaptation was planned with the first installment debuting in March 2012. But these numbers are merely evidence that the books captured people's attention. They do not explain why they moved us so deeply.

The Hunger Games is a series that gets inside you and holds your imagination captive. Even after I finished the books, the story and the characters haunted my thoughts. I couldn't let them go. And it wasn't enough to simply re-read the series (although I did that too, multiple times); these were stories that meant something, stories that dealt with themes larger than themselves, and I needed to let those themes speak into my life. As I reflected upon The Hunger Games, I realized that I shouldn't have been so quick to postpone reading them in favor of theology and Christian living books. Although not explicitly "Christian" books, the themes explored in The Hunger Games are the same ones Christians have wrestled with since the days of Jesus and his apostles. Themes of love, compassion, and justice in the face of oppression. Themes of what it looks like to live full of the hope that a better world is possible.

Amidst the excitement of a well-told story, The Hunger Games addresses those hard questions that people in our culture can't help but ask—questions not simply about why there is evil in the world (because we all already know it's there), but questions about how to respond to that evil. People aren't interested in theoretical musings that have no relevancy; they want to know how injustice can end and lives can be improved *now*. They want to know whether their core beliefs have anything to say to the realities of oppression, violence, and economic inequalities that continually confront them, and whether they can do anything about those problems. Therefore, when readers encounter in the pages of The Hunger Games a story of exactly that sort, it resonates with some of their deepest questions and longings. But as I realized, these are also the questions Jesus addressed as he called and instructed people in how to follow the ways of the Kingdom of God. Jesus didn't come offering spiritual advice meant only for some elusive future realm; he offered people a tangible way to live transformatively every day. So, while The Hunger Games is not a retelling of the Christian story, I found in it a helpful and vivid portrayal of both the struggles and blessings of pursuing the sort of life that can't help but turn the world upside-down.

Hence this book. To explore the intersection of The Hunger Games and the Gospel is to discover echoes of the good news in the pages of these young adult science fiction books. The good news that Jesus taught of the Kingdom of God offered tangible ways that a world full of injustice and oppression can be transformed into one of hope. This was a message of good news back when Jesus first preached it and still is for us today. And it's a message that resonates throughout the imaginative narrative of The Hunger Games. The Hunger Games is not the Gospel, or even an allegory of the Gospel story, but it reflects the good news, helping to illuminate the path of Kingdom living for readers today.

But before I dive into its themes, here are a few things you might need to know about the books, starting with a few disclaimers.

This book explores the themes in The Hunger Games novels. I'm sure the films will delve into most of the same themes, but books are always far more nuanced than their film versions. If you haven't read all the books, let me give fair warning of spoilers. It should also go without saying that the following summary is a poor substitute for the brilliance of the actual books, so if I were you, I'd just drop everything and go read the series right now. Seriously. But for those of you who haven't read the books repeatedly like I have, let me give a brief reminder of what they're all about.

Spoiler Alert! The Hunger Games tells the story of Katniss Everdeen and her struggle to survive in the post-apocalyptic and totalitarian country of Panem, the North America of the distant future. At some point war and environmental disaster destroyed the United States, and out of the remnants grew the new country of Panem. The nation consists of a wealthy Capitol city, located in the Rocky Mountain region, with twelve poorer districts surrounding it. There was at one time a thirteenth district, but it was supposedly destroyed by the Capitol during a rebellion some seventy-five years prior to the events in the books.

Like any totalitarian regime, the Capitol asserts complete control over the districts, forcing the people there to abide by strict rules and work in industries that supply the needs of the Capitol. And predictably, while the Capitol is a luxurious, technologically advanced society, the districts are destitute and struggling. Nevertheless, the Capitol demands utter compliance from the districts and ensures it by keeping a military presence in each one. It also exerts its control by reminding the people of the price of rebellion by selecting two children from each district every year as "tributes" to be sacrificed in the Hunger Games—a televised spectacle that plays like a mash-up between *Survivor* and *Gladiator*. Cherished as the height of entertainment in the Capitol, the Games are required viewing in the districts where families and friends must watch their children fight to the death.

Readers first meet Katniss on Reaping Day, the day when the children are chosen from the districts to compete. When her younger sister Prim's name is drawn in the District 12 Reaping, Katniss volunteers to take her place in the arena. Joining her from District 12 is Peeta Mellark, the baker's son who had once saved Katniss's life by giving her bread when she was desperately hungry. With their mentor Haymitch Abernathy, the sole District 12 victor from a past Hunger Games, they are taken to the Capitol for complete makeovers, Games training, and to be paraded in front of the adoring Capitol crowds eager to see them get slaughtered. But coming from the poorest of the districts, where winning the Games is nearly unheard of, Katniss and Peeta are automatically different than the average tributes. They don't strive for fame or posture themselves as trained combatants like other tributes, but reflect their humble background in their demeanor, even supporting each other during their presentation. Still, with the help of the spectacular clothing made by her stylist, Cinna, Katniss is presented as "the girl on fire." She becomes a favorite when Peeta admits on live television that he has been in love with her for years.

In the Games Arena, Katniss attempts to survive both the elements and the other tributes. She proves to be a smart contestant, catching food and outsmarting other players. She even teams up with the youngest tribute, little Rue from District 11, and after Rue is brutally murdered Katniss sings to her and covers her body with wildflowers. When, in a twist of the rules, the Gamemakers announce that two players could win the Games that year, Katniss immediately finds Peeta, who has been badly wounded, and helps them both survive to the end. When the earlier rule change is revoked at the last minute, she and Peeta take a gamble and attempt to commit suicide with poisonous berries instead of turning on each other. The Gamemakers relent and allow them both to live, though the Capitol is furious with Katniss for this highly subversive act.

The second book in the series, *Catching Fire*, picks up with Katniss discovering that unless she can convince the Districts that her act with the berries was done only out of love for Peeta (and not as resistance of the Capitol), everyone she loves will get hurt. She tries to appease the Capitol, but soon realizes through her victory tour of the districts that there is widespread unrest. Her actions, and especially the Mockingjay pin she wore in the Arena, have become symbols of rebellion. In response to the stirrings of rebellion, the Capitol uses the Quarter Quell, a glorified version of the Games, to punish the districts by sending past victors of the games back into the arena. Katniss, Peeta, and the friends they made amongst the other victors end up back in the Games, once again fighting for their lives. But an underground plot is afoot in Panem, and when Katniss brings down the forcefield containing the arena with an arrow, rebels in partnership with District 13 (which hadn't been destroyed after all) are there to rescue her.

The third book, *Mockingjay*, finds Katniss living in the underground bunkers of District 13 trying to cope with the fact that the Capitol has captured Peeta and firebombed District 12 into oblivion. She decides to accept the role as the symbol of the rebellion (the Mockingjay) and is soon filming propaganda pieces and, on occasion, directly combating Capitol forces. The deeper she gets into the resistance, though, the more uneasy she becomes with the fact that the rebels and District 13 act much like the Capitol. After infiltrating the Capitol on a mission that goes terribly wrong, Katniss ends up at the president's mansion with the intention to kill him. Instead, she arrives just in time to see her sister, who was sent to help care for the wounded, killed by what were possibly the rebels' own bombs. Thus, after the rebels are victorious and their new president suggests that they hold another Hunger Games with the children of the Capitol leaders as tributes, Katniss makes a bold move. As the Mockingjay, she has been selected to execute the Capitol's President Snow, but chooses to shoot the new president instead, ending that new reign before it can even begin. Declared insane, Katniss is sent back to District 12 to help rebuild it from the ashes. There, she must mourn what she has lost and slowly piece together a way to live in the new world she helped create.

Katniss's path of trying to figure out how to take those tentative steps forward into a new world resonates with readers who are also trying to make sense of their own world because it sets Katniss's journey apart from other similar stories. She doesn't get to click her heels together or push through a wardrobe at the end of the journey to find she has returned to the safety and comforts of home. Nor does she have the peace of Harry Potter's concluding "all was well" or the chance to echo Edward and Bella's continuing "blissfully into this small but perfect piece of our forever." For Katniss there is no going back, no returning home to pick up where she left off before her adventures began. Her world has completely changed and, in her brokenness, she has to hold together the pieces of what is left in a way that makes living possible. But the way forward isn't one of hopeless despair. Living in the new world is difficult, requiring change and growth, but it isn't impossible. It's just that the struggle to end oppression and build a better world is complicated and messy—which is the sort of honest yet hopeful message that speaks to the lives of readers.

The Power of Stories

Because of such themes, The Hunger Games fits into the recent popular trend in young adult literature of presenting dystopian as opposed to utopian realities. For most of the 20th century, that genre's analysis of human societies generally had happy endings. As in a Disney fairytale, the bad guys would be vanquished, a perfect society formed, and everyone would supposedly live happily-ever-after. But since the end of the Cold War and the beginning of the so-called "War on Terror," it's been hard to sell such black-and-white views of the world. Many supposed utopias themselves suppressed justice and freedom, making naïve solutions no longer an option for speculative fictions. Hence the rise of dystopian fictions which "present for the first time bleak analyses of human society without promise of the euphoric ending which is usually expected in that literature."[1]

Popular books like *The Giver* and *The Uglies* series, and shows like *The Matrix*, *The Dark Knight*, and *Battlestar Galactica* portray such struggling societies. Not that these stories assume a better world is not possible, they just don't prescribe an idea of utopia as a fixed end in itself. They instead leave it up to the readers to do the hard work of imagining a way forward. Since 9/11, when even the United States could no longer be conceived of as a safe home to return to, the dystopian genre has exploded.

Some, in an attempt at less bleak terminology, have rebranded this emerging genre of literature "transformative utopianism" because it "carr[ies] out important social, cultural, and political work by challenging and reformulating ideas about power and identity, community, the body, spacio-temporal change, and ecology" in order to help readers imagine a better world.[2] It leaves open the possibility that injustice and oppression can be overcome, but acknowledges that the process will be messy, fraught with hardships, and, by nature, ever-changing and fluid. Yet for many this sort of literature represents the only honest way of imaginatively responding to the injustices in our society. Books like The Hunger Games trilogy create space for conversations about oppressive systems in our world, and plant seeds of hope that there are different ways to exist in the world—difficult as they may be.

But of course, stories have always been the best way to pose challenging questions about the world around us. While at times some find it necessary to disguise their critique of the powers that be in fictional guise, stories also have the ability to connect with people on a deeper level. We are drawn to stories because our lives are stories—unfolding narratives of groups of people trying to live as best they can in the world. Like Katniss, we are trying to make sense of the pieces and build a better world with them.

Jesus knew the power of story as he spread the message of the Kingdom of God.[3] He didn't spout off theological formulae, or list the "7 Steps for Living in the Kingdom." He came telling stories.

From crafting parables to revealing poignant glimpses of the Kingdom in the Beatitudes, Jesus drew his listeners into imaginative pictures of what living in the ways of God looked like. The freedom of stories allowed him to safely comment on the current socio-political situation of his time and then illustrate how an alternate social order might value people far differently. To those living under the oppressive regime of the Roman Empire, these stories presented ways of being in the world that allowed even the marginalized and the poor to reclaim their identity as children of God.

Jesus's stories told of a Kingdom that is among us and yet is not of this world. As author Brian McLaren explains, that means that the "kingdom is very much in this world, but it doesn't work the way earthly kingdoms or empires do."[4] To a people used to centuries of living under the exile, manipulation, and oppression of conquering empires, Jesus's stories demonstrated that empires don't have to define who they are. To illustrate this, he wove tales that reminded people of their identity as followers of God and encouraged them to define themselves by that identity instead of the one imposed upon them by Rome. People created in the image of God should reflect that image in their daily lives.

His wasn't some pie-in-the-sky-when-you-die message of escapist hope, but a means of living according to God's ways in the here and now. It was a picture of how people could participate in God's will being done on earth as in heaven, or, as some have referred to it, of allowing God's dreams to come true in the day-to-day tangible reality of life. It also wasn't about forcefully establishing God's Kingdom through the application of human ingenuity or violent revolt, for although God will fully inaugurate the Kingdom someday, it is in living in the ways of God right now that the Kingdom is ours. It is both yet to come and here for us already when we choose to accept the discipline of Jesus's alternative way of being in the world.

Despite that call to live differently, we still live in a broken world where injustice and oppression are the norm. A world where children are kidnapped and forced into sex slavery. Where some women risk having acid thrown in their face every time they dare to show up at school. Where governments court the favor of corporations by allowing them to ignore minimum wage or environmental protection standards. Where a mom can work two jobs and still not be able to afford nutritious food or health care for her kids. Where every 3.6 seconds someone dies from lack of food.

Our world is much like Panem, where the wealth and comfort of the few in the Capitol is provided through the oppression of the districts. Where having the latest toys, instant everything, and the fashions of the moment (at the cheapest possible prices) are more important to some than the lives of the people who suffer to supply them. Where protecting a political ideology and hoarding one's wealth are higher priorities than feeding the hungry. Such a world is obviously not a realization of God's dreams. And sadly, Christians, especially in countries like the United States, are often seduced into living in the ways of the world that devalue the image of God in others. Many Christians have forgotten how to live in the world in ways that are not of the world. What Jesus delivered as a transforming message of hope has been spiritualized away to nothing more than pithy sayings or pleasing rituals designed to make us feel content as we live in the ways of the world. But for those who know that life is not as it was meant to be, stories like The Hunger Games serve as reminders of what it looks like to choose a different path.

To that end, this book seeks to explore the good news in Jesus's stories about living in the way of the Kingdom of God by looking at the example of similar stories in The Hunger Games. Each chapter takes one of the rich statements of the Beatitudes, which serve as mini-pictures of God's dreams realized on earth as in heaven, and reflects on how those pictures are exhibited in the narrative of The Hunger Games. The chapter then examines the significance of each Beatitude within the setting of Jesus's own time as well as the truth it reveals for living in the way of Jesus amidst the present realities of our own society.

The early followers of Christ had hope because they knew which dreams to value as they lived into the Kingdom. They knew to grasp hold of the dreams that manifested the ways of compassion and love, self-sacrifice and gentleness, respect and inclusion. In the face of oppression, they chose to declare their allegiance to the realization of these dreams instead. Like Katniss, they had their lives turned upside down and had to grow and change as people. But that's what the transformation Jesus talked about involves—becoming new creations who can no longer exist under the old ways of the world, but who instead embrace the life-affirming ways of the Kingdom of God. That is the life Christians are called to—a life that, despite struggle and hardship, still chooses to work for a better world that reflects God's dreams.

Thankfully, we have stories to help show us the way. These are stories that spark our imaginations and teach us how to ensure the stories our children tell are more about justice and compassion than oppression and greed. These are stories that are more than just stories, but which also serve as avatars of hope as they engage our minds in ceaseless imaginative play about how to build a better world.

Stories like Katniss's. Like The Hunger Games.

So let our imaginations play, and let the games begin.

Chapter One
The Poor in Spirit: Living in the United States of Panem

"Blessed are the poor in spirit, for theirs is the kingdom of heaven."
~ Matthew 5:3

Starving to Death in Safety

In the summer of 2010, my husband Mike spent time helping to build schools in Marfranc, Haiti with a group from our church. As they walked through the village one afternoon, a young man and woman approached them and begged them to take their baby. In a country where having a tin roof (as opposed to leaves) on your shack is a sign of wealth, where food is hard to come by even if you have money, and the jobs to earn money are non-existent, this couple saw giving away their child as the most loving thing they could do. My husband said his group was literally too stunned to respond. No amount of relief work preparation or keeping up with world news can prepare a person from the richest nation in the world for poverty so dire that people would give away their children in an attempt to save them from it.

Yet, while Haiti (especially post-earthquake) may be the poorest country in the world, hunger and deprivation are more common in this world than not. We live in a world where one out of every seven people will go to bed hungry tonight. Hunger remains the world's number one health risk, killing more people each year than AIDS, malaria, and tuberculosis combined. But statistics can't convey the emotional toll that accompanies extreme poverty and ceaseless hunger. Or the way hunger crushes the spirit, slowly extinguishing hope.

Readers of The Hunger Games encounter this sort of soul-crushing poverty in the descriptions of the districts in Panem. District 12 is located in what was once Appalachia, which, even in our own world, is plagued by poverty and its related issues. With coal mining still its main industry, 12 is populated with hunched over men and women who have long since given up trying to cleanse themselves of the ubiquitous coal dust. They live in ramshackle houses with no hot water, and if they're lucky they get a couple of hours of electricity a day. A high electric fence, ostensibly for their security, pens them in, keeping most of them from accessing the bounty of the forest. Broken, downtrodden, and hungry, District 12 is "Where you can starve to death in safety."[5] But, as Katniss later discovers, the dilapidated homes in District 12 look like mansions compared to the shacks the agricultural workers of District 11 live in. And the only occasionally electrified fence in 12 is nothing compared to the 35-foot barbed wire fence complete with watchtowers that surrounds District 11. Poverty, hunger, and oppression are the norm for the districts in Panem.

Even though the situations in the districts might not be as extreme as in places like Haiti, the toll that constant hunger and poor living conditions take on the spirit is the same anywhere. In the districts, life is all about survival—spending what little time and energy one has trying to scrape together enough food to stay alive. Before being sent to the Hunger Games, most of Katniss's life was consumed with acquiring food. Similarly, women and young girls in our world too must spend hours every day walking miles to get water or gather firewood to cook over. Doing so is not only exhausting and dangerous, as they often encounter wild animals and violent men, but the daily task prevents them from caring for their family, getting an education, or having time for a job. Poverty and hunger are all-consuming.

When Jesus delivered the Beatitudes in his Sermon on the Mount, it was to people similarly struggling simply to survive in the day to day. Biblical scholars and historians have determined that most of Jesus's early followers were the poor of the land. Many of them had lost their ancestral lands as the crippling

Roman taxes and Jewish temple taxes sent them spiraling deeper and deeper into debt. They worked for minimal pay as tenant farmers or day laborers on the very lands they used to own.[6] Their spirits had been crushed; what little energy they had left was spent trying to survive. Like those in District 12, they were the poor in spirit, the ones who had given up on hope. Like millions in the world today, they went to bed hungry each night in their ramshackle homes. They were the last people one would ever refer to as blessed, but that was exactly what Jesus did. He said they were blessed because the Kingdom of God was theirs. As absurd as it sounded, that statement gave to them, some for the very first time, that elusive thing called hope.

How Despicable We Must Seem to You

In comparison to the districts, the Capitol of Panem is the epitome of excess. Full of tall rainbow-hued buildings, shiny cars, and well-fed people with eccentric and expensive tastes in clothing and cosmetic enhancements, the Capitol has everything the districts lack. Especially food. When Katniss, straight from the survival mentality of District 12, gets her first taste of the Capitol lifestyle, she is astounded by the ability to push a button and get whatever food she desires. She sees a basket of rolls on the breakfast table and thinks on how it could keep her family going for a week. While in District 12 parents brought their emaciated children to Katniss's healer mother who would prescribe the only thing the parents couldn't give—more food— citizens of the Capitol hold lavish feasts complete with a drink that helps them throw up so they can gorge on more.

Not unlike in the United States today, the Capitol is described as a place where people surgically alter themselves to appear thinner or more fashionable. While in the districts all around them people die because they cannot afford food, people in the Capitol spend money on trivial body modifications like dying their skin green or implanting cat whiskers on their faces. Far from obsessing with looking thinner or younger, in District

12 Katniss explains that old-age is seen as a remarkable accomplishment and plumpness envied as a sign of success. Without the abundance of affluence, life is valued differently. The struggle to survive makes being alive that much more precious. But excess is the norm in the Capitol, where citizens have the time and resources to spend on luxuries and trivialities. When Cinna, Katniss's aware and understanding stylist, observes her shocked reaction to these extremes of the Capitol, all he can do is comment sadly, "How despicable we must seem to you."[7]

Those of us who are used to having our next meal pretty much guaranteed have a hard time understanding how we are seen through the eyes of others. I recall a missionary trying to explain to an uninterested suburban youth group how she came to finally understand how those struggling with hunger view the excesses of American lifestyles. She shared that while serving in the barrios in Mexico, she had helped put on a Vacation Bible School for children. Pulling from her American playbook, one afternoon she involved the kids in an over-the-top mess-fest of water balloons and flour bombs. It was only afterward, when she saw a young boy attempting to scoop up the fallen flour mixed in with the dirt to take home and eat, that she realized how blind she had been. In a society of excess, food can be thrown away as a toy; but there she was, supposedly a representative of Jesus Christ, mocking the children's hunger by tossing precious food in the dirt.

Studies show that in the United States, we waste some 40 percent of all of our food. That means we end up throwing away perfectly good food. That sort of excessive waste is the luxury of those who have never wondered where their next meal will come from, who don't understand the message those actions send to those desperately trying to survive. Like most of the citizens in the Capitol who had no clue why their excess would appear cruel and offensive to people from the districts, most in the missionary's audience that evening weren't ready to hear her words. They couldn't fathom why the needs of others should affect their right to have whatever sort of fun they desired whenever they wanted. Unlike both this missionary and

Katniss's stylist Cinna, but very much like most citizens of the Capitol, they lacked the ability to see the world through others' eyes.

If You Lift a Finger, We Will Destroy You

Of course, the struggle to survive isn't merely against poverty and hunger, but against the systems that cause those conditions. Large gaps between the excessively rich and the extremely poor do not happen by chance. They are typically the result of oppressive practices that subjugate the masses for the benefit of the few. The poor in spirit were more than just the downtrodden and the hungry; they were the oppressed. Jesus didn't deliver the Beatitudes to the elite and the powerful; he spoke directly to the poor who were living under Roman oppression. In Roman times, just as in our day and in the world of The Hunger Games, the excessive abundance of the privileged must come from somewhere. Someone must be footing the bill for lavish lifestyles. Unfortunately, it is the poorest of the poor who end up paying those costs by sending tribute to the powerful nations who forcefully extract what the destitute can't afford to give.

This world of oppression is the only world Katniss ever knew. She was born into a society where the Capitol rules the districts with an iron fist. Not only must the people work in their district's prescribed industry—coal mining in 12, agriculture in 11, or fishing in 4, for example—but they must do so on behalf of the Capitol. Quotas must be met and the fruits of their labor go to provide for the Capitol. In District 12, workers must use their meager income to choose between buying food or the coal they dig up all day to warm their homes. In District 11, amidst a plethora of food, people starve and yet are publicly beaten if they dare taste the food they labor to grow. Compliance is enforced by Capitol-trained "Peacekeepers" who mete out punishments and executions to those who fail to obey. When Katniss's best friend Gale is caught trying to sell a turkey he has hunted illegally, he's publicly whipped to the point of death. Peace, meaning only absence of rebellion, is kept through intimidation, fear, and the weariness of a hungry and exhausted population.

To further remind the districts of the Capitol's power, the districts must also send their children as tributes to the Hunger Games each year. At the annual Reaping, every child between 12 and 18 has his or her name entered into the Hunger Games drawing. In exchange for more entries into the drawing, the poor are allowed to sign up for tesserae—meager allotments of food provided each month by the Capitol. Entries are cumulative and up to the number of people in one's family can be taken out. So the more desperate the parents are, the higher the likelihood their children will be the ones chosen to be slaughtered in the Hunger Games. As Katniss comments, with a system like that it's hard not to resent those who have a little more and don't have to sign up for tesserae, even as she admits that the system is just the Capitol's way of keeping the people in the Districts divided and distrustful of one another.

The system of oppression presented in The Hunger Games is modeled on the tactics used in the Roman Empire. Tribute and tesserae were common practices used by the Romans to keep their ever-expanding empire under their thumb. Roman citizens whose jobs had been outsourced to conquered slaves were granted tesserae, or coins that they could exchange for bread. The famous *Pax Romana*, where "peace" was maintained by quelling uprisings through intimidation and fear, enabled the Romans to extract tribute from the peoples they had conquered. With vast amounts of the food and wealth they produced going to pay the Romans, occupied peoples sank deeper and deeper into poverty.

Jesus, of course, was born into this setting of Roman occupation and oppression. When in the nativity story in Luke we read of the Roman Emperor conducting a census that requires all peoples to return to their ancestral lands, what we are really reading about is the tribute system at work. In Jewish culture, land was not bought and sold (although it could be lost to debtors) but belonged to one's ancestral line. Joseph apparently had been unable to scratch out a living on his family lands and so had left to try to make it as a carpenter. That is, until the Roman Empire declared that all people must return to their land so that the Emperor could be sure to extract as much tribute as possible from the people he conquered. It can be easy to forget when hearing the Christmas story that Jesus was not born to the elite or the powerful. His family was lower class and oppressed. Even a very pregnant woman had no choice but to obey the Empire and travel to Bethlehem where her son would be born in the muck of a stable and laid to sleep in a feeding trough. This is how the poor in spirit are born.

Questioning the Roman system of oppression resulted in death. For instance, around the time of Jesus's birth the Romans responded to Jewish acts of rebellion in the Galilee region (like their refusal to pay tribute to the pagan gods of Rome) by slaughtering and enslaving tens of thousands of people. In 4 B.C.E., the Romans burned the town of Sepphoris (just a few miles from Jesus's boyhood home in Nazareth) to the ground, enslaving all its inhabitants.[8] We see similar acts of oppression in The Hunger Games. After the Quarter Quell games and Katniss's subversive act of bringing down the force field, the Capitol retaliates against her district. No one in the town responds to her televised action with either protest or celebration, and yet within minutes Capitol hoverplanes were ruthlessly firebombing the district. Like the Romans did to Sepphoris, the Capitol burned District 12 to the ground for daring to produce someone who challenged their absolute control.

Under such tight-fisted rule, the people in the districts aren't even allowed to speak against the Capitol's regime. Questioning the Reaping system that sends their children to be slaughtered is forbidden, as is complaining about the tribute system that leaves them poor and hungry. Dreaming of a better world out loud can only get them in trouble, so most people give up on hope and allow fear to lead to compliance. Katniss describes learning the danger of subversive words as a child—"I learned to hold my tongue and to turn my features into an indifferent mask so that no one could ever read my thoughts. Do my work quietly in school. Make only polite small talk in the public market."[9]

The message of the Capitol to the districts is clear: we can take your children with impunity and "If you lift a finger, we will destroy every last one of you."[10] Oppression crushes hope in whatever way it can—through lack of resources, denial of freedoms, and the threat of violence. This is Katniss's world in The Hunger Games, it was Jesus's world under Rome, and it is the lived experience of people all over the world today.

It is, for instance, the experience of the families in the North Kivu Province of Congo's eastern mining districts. Since the mines near their homes contain precious minerals essential for high-end technology items like smart phones and laptops, they end up living in fear as terrorist groups compete for control of those lucrative minerals. In the summer of 2010, guerilla soldiers sought to control these villages by rounding up and systematically gang-raping the women, children, and even babies in front of their family members.[11] Resources that could have helped revitalize their communities are now the reason for their oppression as they try to survive under constant fear.

It is the experience of the people in Burma. In a country where one in every three children is malnourished, the excessively rich ruling military junta steadily raised prices on essential items like food and gasoline. When the people, led by Buddhist monks, raised their voices in nonviolent protest against such injustices in the summer of 2007, they were swiftly and harshly dealt with by the military. Even providing food and water to the protesting monks resulted in a prison sentence.[12]

It is the experience of countless people in countries crippled by debt payments—countries like Haiti, along with many others. Stipulations imposed by the IMF and World Bank to repay loans made to dictators years ago force countries to send far more money in interest payments and subsidies to rich lending nations than they have to spend on education and medical systems in their own countries.[13] The people are powerless to speak out against this foreign demand for tribute, but the hardships of their everyday life attest to its effects.

It is even the experience of many in the United States, where we are often trained to believe such oppression does not exist. I met a Native American woman who lives on the streets in my hometown of Austin, Texas. She told me that she is regularly rounded up by immigration police and held until they finally allow her to prove that she is a U.S. citizen. Apparently having dark skin and being homeless is enough cause to deny her freedom. Many fear that harassment like this is becoming increasingly more common as states and municipalities work to pass laws restricting freedoms as they make racial profiling essentially mandatory.

Hunger, poverty, poor health, fear, violence and lack of freedoms are not just elements of fiction, but daily realities in our world. In light of such realities, consider the emotional (and political) impact Jesus must have had when he showed up in Nazareth, a region with a long history of oppression, and proclaimed that he had come to fulfill Isaiah's prophetic words by releasing the captives and setting the oppressed free. Those words would have been charged with meaning for people living in fear under the Roman tribute system just as they are for people desperate for liberation today. Oppression orchestrates compliance by crushing all hope. Yet Jesus came offering hope and the blessing of the Kingdom of God to those whose spirits had been broken.

Panem et Circenses

Like the well-fed and constantly entertained citizens of Panem's Capitol, those of us who live in the relative luxury of North America are too often woefully ignorant of the oppression in the world around us. We are so distracted by our entertainment—sports, reality TV, the latest sensational trial, and all the rest—and so isolated in our comfortable lives that we never have an opportunity to get to know the poor in spirit or the oppression that shapes their experience. And while this ignorance might explain a good deal of our inability to understand the needs and the perspectives of the poor and oppressed, it is even more difficult for those in positions of privilege to sympathize with the suffering when it is often our own excesses that cause (or at least prevent us from stopping) that very suffering.

When confronted with the stories of oppression mentioned above, one has to wonder why more people don't speak out against the oppression. Surely in the Roman Empire there were some who weren't starving or enslaved, or who perhaps had some influence and could have served as advocates for the hurting. Sadly, however, as Jesus's parable of the Good Samaritan subversively illustrates, the elite members of those societies could not be counted on to show neighborly love to the broken. The Priest and the Levite in that story, whose positions of religious leadership set them apart from the average person struggling to survive, pass by the wounded man, too consumed with their own concerns to be bothered with his predicament. The same was true of many Roman citizens—especially those in positions of power amongst conquered peoples. The Romans ensured their compliance through the policy famously known as "bread and circuses."

The idea of bread and circuses is simple. While the Romans used force and fear to keep conquered peoples under control, they kept their own people controlled through the distractions of bread and circuses. The practice of tesserae kept the people's bellies full (who's going to complain about the government when they feed you?) but the term had another meaning as well. Tesserae weren't just the coins one exchanged for food; they were also the tickets (coins stamped with seat numbers) to the arenas. In other words, tesserae could be exchanged for both bread and circuses.

While the bread kept the citizens of Rome satiated and placated, the circuses kept them distracted. From theatrical performances to horse races to gladiator games where slaves were forced to fight each other or wild animals to the death, the games entertained the masses. Politicians would distribute bread or host games to win the favor of the population. It was in frustration at this shallowness among his fellow Romans that the 1st-century C.E. satirist Juvenal coined the phrase *"panem et circenses"* (bread and circuses) to mock those who were too distracted to care about justice or the needs of the oppressed.

The handful of Hunger Games readers who happened to take Latin in high school would have been clued in that the series was directly referencing the bread and circuses of ancient Rome. Early on, we read that the country itself is named Panem (bread) and has a tesserae system that provided the districts both food and a higher chance at a ticket to the games (but as participants, not as spectators). In the final book Plutarch, the ex-Head Gamemaker turned rebel, explains to Katniss that citizens of the Capitol have given up their political power and responsibilities for *"Panem et Circenses"* – to remain well-fed and entertained.

The people in the Capitol can gorge themselves on gourmet foods, have the latest electronics, and obsess over a game show where children fight to the death. The people of Panem must (under threat of death) send the fruit of their labor as well as their children to provide for the insatiable consumerism of the Capitol. Their suffering, starvation, and brokenness supplies the bread and circuses that keep the citizens of the Capitol diverted enough to not care about the hidden costs of their lifestyle.

The comparisons to our modern world couldn't be more obvious. In the United States, our consumptive lifestyle similarly comes at the expense of suffering people around the world. Like Rue and her family, who work in the agricultural District 11, many of the workers who grow our produce face dangerous working conditions, are paid far less than minimum wage, and regularly face abuse from their supervisors. Our clothes are often sewn in sweatshops where young girls who are desperate for any job at all work illegally long hours for pittance pay and regularly face verbal, physical, and sexual abuse that they must keep silent about for fear of losing their jobs. The poor in our present-day Appalachia are subjected to hazardous conditions and illness-causing toxic pollution from the common practices of mountaintop removal mining and fracking (a hazardous practice in natural gas extractions) to give us energy. And the cost of keeping down the prices on our everyday luxuries, items like chocolate and coffee, for instance, is workers being denied living wages and children being forced into slavery.[14] In these instances and more, we can see that the economic and political systems of our own world are structured in much the same way as those of Panem. The labor and produce and very lives of the many are controlled and redirected so that a relative few can live like kings. And in our world today, those few are *us*—those of us who live in a society where even the middle class, struggling though many of us are, are still among the wealthiest, healthiest, and most powerful people ever to exist in human history.

Our consumerist lifestyle comes at a price, and it is the poor in spirit around the world who are paying it. They are the ones sacrificing to provide us bread, but we're the ones too distracted by our circuses to care about their suffering. From the latest bands and newest iWhatever to our favorite sports teams and reality television, we have become a culture obsessed with being continually entertained. According to the U.S. Department of Labor, the average person spends about three hours every day watching television. That's nearly a full day out of every week, or a solid month and a half out of every year. Assuming a sixty-five-year lifespan, that's over eight years of our lives spent watching television.

Now, don't get me wrong. I'm not saying entertainment is bad (more on this later). I'm a huge fan of good stories (like The Hunger Games) and yes, even reality television. But when our passion for who will win the big game or be crowned the latest Top Chef, Biggest Loser, or Survivor exceeds our passion for helping others, something is wrong. We know our circuses mean more to us than the needs of others when we can't fathom spending the same amount of time serving those others that we would gladly spend standing in line for U2 tickets or voting each week for our favorite American Idol contestant. We know it when it turns out that the only time we are really moved to compassion is during horrible natural disasters—earthquakes in Haiti, hurricanes on the Gulf Coast, nuclear meltdowns in

Japan—when our sick voyeurism glues us to the unfolding images of horror on-screen.

It's like when Katniss was sent to the Hunger Games for the first time. There she encountered an unnatural fire followed by a barrage of firebombs and quickly realized that the Gamemakers had sent them because the game had gotten too boring, no deaths or fights at all that day. In a culture that has exchanged its responsibility to help build a better world for the opiate of our circuses, we expect even our news stories to be sensationalized and entertaining. After the initial shocking tragedy of the earthquakes in Haiti and Japan, or the devastation of Katrina and the BP oil spill, we quickly lose interest in a now "dull" story and demand something new. The continued suffering in the aftermath, and the long, slow process of struggling to rebuild amidst the ever-present oppression of bureaucracies, isn't interesting enough to capture our attention.

But the Kingdom of God is all about working toward a better world in slow ways and small steps. This pursuit is not based on some misguided dream of utopia, or a misplaced faith in human progress, but is from Jesus's teaching us to pray that the ways of God's Kingdom will be manifest "on earth as they are in heaven." Jesus told the poor in spirit that the blessings of the Kingdom were already theirs to live into. Not in the kind of 60-minute extreme makeover that our entertainment-obsessed culture seems to expect, but through the slow and faithful habit of living into the ways of the Kingdom—ways of justice, compassion, reconciliation, and self-giving love. It is through choosing to join Jesus on his mission to set the oppressed free and bring good news to the poor. Building a better world isn't some pipe dream about the next stage in human evolution, but the natural and tangible outcome of people actually living in this way of Jesus. But to make claim to that promise in reality, we must let go of our bread and circuses and commit to the discipline of standing in solidarity with the poor in spirit.

The Question Is, What Are You Going to Do?

Katniss was always a fighter. After her father's death in the mines and her mother's subsequent descent into extreme depression brought her already poor family to the brink of starvation, she came close to losing all hope. Looking back, she acknowledges that if she had been older than 11 at the time, she probably would have had to sell herself just so they could eat. Instead, she learned to hunt. Recalling the lessons her father taught her about edible plants and how to snare and shoot wild game, she now ventures out past the security fence to keep her family alive. Of course, in District 12 it is illegal to go outside the fence, illegal to hunt, and even more illegal to possess a weapon. Katniss knows that she could be publicly executed for hunting, but as she and her hunting partner Gale agree that death from a Capitol bullet to the head would be quicker and far preferable to dying of hunger.

In the face of oppression, Katniss does what she has to in order to survive. She uses that same strategy during the Hunger Games as well. When she forces the Capitol's hand by making the Gamemakers choose between having no victor or allowing both her and Peeta to win, survival becomes even more difficult. People see her gamble with the berries as an act of defiance against the Capitol and turn her into a symbol of resistance. To protect the ones she loves, she tries, for a time, to do the Capitol's bidding by discouraging rebellion in whatever ways she can, but she soon realizes that oppressors don't work that way. The Capitol decides to tighten its grip on her district, leading to more hardships for everyone. And then it sends the Hunger Games victors back to the arena for the Quarter Quell.

Held every twenty-five years, the Quarter Quell is a glorified version of the Hunger Games intended to drive home to the Districts the cost of rebellion. For the 75th Quarter Quell, the participants are chosen from existing victors in order to remind the districts that even their strongest members are no match for the Capitol. Katniss and Peeta are thus sent back into the arena.

Katniss recognizes this latest act of oppression for what it is—an attempt to destroy even the slightest vestiges of hope in the districts. As she comments, the victors, having escaped both the arena and the subtle noose of crushing poverty, "are the very embodiment of hope where there is no hope. And now twenty-three of us will be killed to show that even that hope was an illusion."[15]

But the Quarter Quell is the last straw for many of the districts. Instead of being cowed by the Capitol, some launch a full-scale rebellion and orchestrate Katniss's escape from the games. In retaliation, the Capitol tortures those of her allies who weren't able to escape the arena and firebombs District 12 into the ground. In response to these acts of oppression, Gale asks Katniss, "The question is, what are you going to do?" to which she voices her intention to become the Mockingjay—the persona the rebels created around her as a symbol of resistance to the Capitol.[16]

She accepts her role as this symbol of hope for the people, dangerous though it may be. By simply being herself and making sacrifices to help those around her, she demonstrates a way to respond to the Capitol's oppressive acts and sparks in people's imaginations the possibility of a better world. Discontent broods silently in oppressed peoples, but it takes the creative imagination of a leader with nothing left to lose to provide a symbol of hope that people will follow. Like a Gandhi or a Martin Luther King Jr., Katniss becomes that symbol to help the people of Panem break the chains of injustice.

It is this re-imagining of the unjust ways of the world that the Kingdom of God is all about. Jesus said to the poor whose spirits had been crushed by years of oppression that the blessings of the Kingdom were already theirs. There was another way of living in the world than the way of Rome—a joyous existence where people care for each other's needs, as opposed to a world where the elite few oppress the masses for their own selfish gain or keep them placated with nothing but bread and circuses. A blessed way of life where slaves are seen as brothers, children welcomed, and even women were invited to learn at the feet of the rabbi. A subversive way of life in which, when your oppressor slaps you on your right cheek (a backhanded hit given to inferiors), you do not cower in fear or retaliate in anger, but turn your other cheek, forcing him to treat you like an equal by then hitting you with his fist.[17] In a world where oppression thrives on strict hierarchies and fear, the ways of the Kingdom turned everything upside down.

People flocked to Jesus to hear about this way of life that challenged the absolutizing power that was Rome. His words gave the poor in spirit dignity and, more importantly, hope. People started living out this subversive way of life. They took care of the sick and needy in their midst, ensuring that their widows and orphans were always cared for. History confirms that the early Christians were living in the ways of God's Kingdom instead of Rome's. In a letter to the Roman Emperor in 111 C.E., Pliny the Younger describes the need to increase the persecution of the Christians because their subversive ways were undermining the Roman economic system.[18] These Christians truly believed that they could trust in God and not the unjust practices of Rome to supply their daily bread. By declaring their allegiance to the Kingdom of God instead of Rome, they made the empire uneasy.

Katniss too comes to realize the Capitol's fragile dependence on the resources they exploit from the districts – food, energy, even the manpower for their peacekeeping force. Without the docile acquiescence of the districts, the Capitol's power would quickly evaporate. The Capitol knows this just like Rome did, and just like the purveyors of power in our own world today still know. Absolutist systems cannot abide dissent and will do whatever they can to remain in power—either by tightening their grip or, more subtly but far more effectively, by convincing citizens that they can't live without their bread and circuses. When we are told that rocking the boat and upsetting the system will endanger all those things that we believe keep us secure and happy, we are much less inclined to take a stand for justice. This makes living in the ways of the Kingdom, although joyous, hard—especially for those used to having it all. Jesus knew this when he called the poor in spirit blessed for having the Kingdom, but said it might be easier for a camel to go through the eye of a needle than for those used to privilege and luxury to actually live in the ways of this Kingdom. Not impossible, just extraordinarily difficult.

In the United States, declaring freedom from a system that benefits us at the expense of others is often too difficult for some. They desire to follow Jesus, but just can't bring themselves to make the sacrifices necessary to love and respect others like Jesus did. It has become common for them to spiritualize away Jesus's words and make the Kingdom about some heavenly future and not about the faithful transformation of their lives starting right now. But, as Jesus demonstrated, the Kingdom of God is all about turning the oppressive ways of the world upside-down. For some that will mean the end of fear and oppression, but for others it will mean ending our ignorance of and involvement in systems that terrorize and oppress. The end result is freedom for both, but only if we choose, like Katniss, to do the hard work of following that path.

The following chapters will explore some of what it might look like to declare our allegiance with the Kingdom of God here in the midst of our own world. They address how we as disciples of Jesus can accept the discipline of living counter-culturally— choosing to love others, free the oppressed, and care for the hurting in our own world. That process isn't easy, but it is blessed. The point of a discipline is that it takes effort and intentionality, and that is even truer of those habits that resist the unjust systems of the world. Katniss discovered that declaring her freedom from the Capitol brought her tremendous pain. And Jesus was accused of inciting rebellion and tortuously executed by Rome for daring to propose a different kind of kingdom. But even his instrument of death became a symbol of hope for those who truly believed that the ways of the Kingdom of God were the most blessed way to live.

Chapter Two
Those Who Mourn: Remembering the Things It Would Be a Crime to Forget

"Blessed are those who mourn, for they will be comforted."
~ Matthew 5:4

Bury the Real Pain

In the summer of 2011, I was privileged to hear legendary civil rights activist Vincent Harding speak on the role of the church in society. As a religious history scholar and former speechwriter for Martin Luther King Jr., Harding has had ample and unique opportunities to observe religion in American culture. As he said in his talk, what he sees in the church these days is pain and suffering. Severe blows have been delivered to the body of Christ from institutional and social evils such as racism and the inequalities it produces, harming both those who commit and those who suffer from those sins. But instead of healing those wounds and embracing the path of reconciliation, the church has often allowed them to linger and fester. As Harding described it, the church hasn't allowed itself to engage in the process of mourning. Instead of facing the truth of the wounds and naming, lamenting, and confessing to injustices, the church tries to ignore the pain—which, as any good doctor would tell you, only makes the injury worse.

There is a power that comes from the process of mourning. Jesus called those engaged in that process blessed because they are the ones who will find comfort to heal their pain. But mourning is dangerous. As Harding mentioned, to even begin mourning societal pain requires that we first name the institutional evils that have caused suffering—an act which those who participate or benefit from such institutions are often reluctant to let happen. Naming cultural sins means someone must take responsibility for those sins and be called to account for them. True repentance involves not only ending one's participation in sin, but working to repair relationships with the people one has harmed. But when the bread and circuses of our luxurious lifestyles and positions of privilege in the world are rooted in the suffering of others, very few have any desire to repent and give up the lives we believe we are entitled to (despite the wounds it causes to our own souls). As scholar and priest Barbara Brown Taylor commented,

> *Repentance begins with the decision to return to relationship: to accept our God-given place in community, and to choose a way of life that increases life for all members of that community. Needless to say, this often involves painful changes, which is why most of us prefer remorse to repentance. We would rather say, "I'm sorry, I'm so sorry, I feel really, really awful about what I have done" than actually start doing things differently.*[19]

So, sadly, when those in power are the source of the suffering, the oppressed must not be allowed to enter into the healing and reconciling process of mourning. And so, as Harding pointed out, instead of making manifest the Kingdom of God on earth as it is in heaven, the body of Christ is suffering.

A similar suffering plagues the districts of Panem. Through years of oppression their pain has multiplied, and there is much that they need to mourn. But letting them mourn is something that the Capitol cannot afford if it is to keep them under strict control. Mourning the children who are chosen on Reaping Day is exactly what the Capitol doesn't want the Districts to do. To mourn would mean tapping into the honest depth of their feelings, being truthful about how devastated they are by the Capitol's actions. Honest feelings that could foster resentment and possible rebellion. So, in the Capitol's eyes, they must not be allowed to mourn.

Instead, the Capitol insists that Reaping Day be treated like a holiday. Everyone gets the day off work and school and the children eligible for the Reaping are expected to dress in their nicest clothes. After the Reaping, the people in the districts are expected to celebrate, and many do, out of relief that their own children have not been chosen this year. But everyone knows it is not a real holiday, even if they are forced to treat it as such. A day of choosing two children from your midst to be slaughtered in the arena is not a day anyone can celebrate. Yet to appease the Capitol, they must go through the motions—a pretense they keep up during the Games as well. The Capitol insists that the Games be treated like a festive sporting event, torturously forcing the districts to cheer on the slaughter of their own. As required viewing for every citizen, the Games cannot be escaped. And neither can they be questioned. This forced celebration projects the illusion that the people somehow support the slaughter of innocents. It is their duty, extracted by force of law, to not only not mourn but actually pretend to enjoy their own oppression.

Even in the arena, Katniss continues to feel the constraint of this expectation. After her ally Rue is murdered, Katniss marks her death by covering Rue's body with wildflowers. Even as she does so, Katniss knows that the Capitol will do their best to avoid showing that act on television. To mourn the death of a fellow tribute is simply too subversive. The arena is a place where the children are sent to fight to the death. It is survival of the fittest, kill or be killed. To feel compassion for another tribute or to mourn his or her death (or to even refer to those deaths as murder) would undermine the control the Capitol has over the districts. Katniss knows that in order to survive in the arena under the Capitol's watchful eye, she has "to bury the real pain" and not allow herself to mourn.[20]

The Romans too knew the power of limiting an oppressed people's ability to mourn. Their favored manner of execution for subversives was crucifixion. Criminals, debtors, insurgents, or simply those they wanted to make an example of were nailed to a cross along well-traveled roads or outside of major towns.

They died slow, agonizing deaths by suffocation, and were left hanging there as their corpses slowly rotted away so that all could see and fear the absolute authority of the Romans. The crucified were not to be buried or given proper rites for the dead—their deaths served as warnings to others, and to mourn them was treason.[21] That Jesus was allowed to be taken off the cross and buried in Joseph of Arimathea's tomb wasn't normal. Someone, probably the well-to-do Joseph, must have coughed up a significant bribe for the right to bury and mourn a convicted criminal.

Present-day governments also know the political importance of preventing people's ability to mourn. In 1991, the U.S. Government reintroduced a law prohibiting images of dead soldiers' coffins from being published by media outlets. Such images allow people to fully comprehend and lament the human cost of war, which could undermine their unwavering support of the government's actions. Even after a legal battle in 2004 forced the U.S. Government to release some images of dead soldiers returning from Iraq, few media outlets dared publish the photographs. The famous British propaganda slogan from World War 2, "Keep Calm and Carry On," is what most governments prefer of their peoples. Don't rock the boat, don't take time to mourn, don't ask questions about injustice—just pretend that everything is normal.

But to actually heal, and not just "carry on," families often need space to mourn publicly over public deaths. When 10-year-old Braydon Nichols' father died when the Chinook helicopter went down in Afghanistan in summer of 2011, he wondered why he wasn't seeing pictures of his father in the news.[22] As his mother explained, Braydon didn't want his father to be just another faceless casualty in a decade long war. So Braydon posted an iReport about his father on CNN, letting people know what a good dad he was. His post generated pages of comments as people helped him honor his father and promised that he would never be forgotten. This public and communal act of mourning was part of what Braydon needed to begin the process of healing and find comfort for his sorrow.

Jesus called those who mourn blessed because they will be comforted. It seems like an obvious thing to say until one considers how often the very act of mourning is restricted. Mourning the freedoms or the lives lost to Roman conquest and oppression was too subversive to be allowed. At times, the Romans even dictated the time a person was allowed to mourn the death of a spouse. The Roman Empire needed people to be married and producing offspring that could serve the needs of the empire, so they set maximum limits on the period one could remain single after the death of a spouse and imposed harsh fines for those who didn't remarry within that timeframe.[23] Mourning, and the comfort it brought, was a luxury Jesus's oppressed audience was not allowed to have. This is why Jesus offered it as a vital part of the upside-down way of life he called the Kingdom of God.

Unless we have the space to mourn, we cannot begin to heal. We can forcefully suppress pain, or attempt to forget painful parts of our communal history, but that just allows the pain to fester and eat away at our souls. Without the ability to mourn, pain can leave us broken.

The Things It Would Be a Crime to Forget

Katniss's emotional development throughout The Hunger Games series illustrates the brokenness that results from an inability to mourn. From being Reaped by the Capitol and then being kept in the public eye both during the Games and later as the symbol of the Rebellion, Katniss is never allowed a chance to mourn. And the list of what she had to mourn is long—the death of her father, her family's struggle to survive, her Reaping, the deaths of the other tributes in her first Games and the Quarter Quell, the destruction of District 12, the deaths of friends during the rebellion, the changes in Peeta and Gale that distanced them from her, and finally the death of her sister Prim. When she is sent back to the remains of District 12 at the end of the series she is broken, burned, and alone. For days on end, all she does is sit in a chair—barely eating, not bathing, not leaving her house. Then, against all odds, her sister's cat turns up, having survived the ravages of the war. Katniss sees him and screams at him to get out since Prim is never coming back, but then, seemingly out of nowhere she starts to weep. Admitting to the reality of her sister's death brought all the wounds and the pain she had been forced to suppress descending down upon her, leaving her with no choice but simply to let the tears fall.

Katniss finally has the chance to mourn, and slowly she begins returning to life. Her healing is slow, and the comfort she finds doesn't change the horrible things that have happened, but it makes living with the memory of those things more bearable. As part of that process of mourning and healing, she and Peeta begin compiling a book to remember the things "it would be a crime to forget."[24] Stories of those who died, the memory of her father's laugh, an image of her sister being licked by the cat. The entries go on and on, and with each one they promise to make the deaths count. Like little Braydon making sure his father's death was remembered, Katniss intuitively knows that telling the stories of what was lost is a vital part of the grieving process.

Yet it is not just the small stories that must be remembered. Remembering the human moments and recognizing the individual sacrifices are vital parts of that process, but so is telling the truth about the societal sins of the past and the acts of oppression in the present. Naming the systems that cause pain and remembering the stories of those who have been hurt not only allows those people's stories to be recognized and mourned, it holds the perpetrators accountable for their actions. There is a comfort in knowing that the people who have hurt you accept responsibility for your pain. There is even greater comfort when they humbly repent of their actions and start the process of reconciliation. But sometimes the best that those in pain can hope for is to ensure that those things it would be a crime to forget are not forgotten. That means telling the truthful, although sometimes difficult and embarrassing, stories of the past.

Katniss had been right about the Capitol not wanting to show the image of Rue's body covered in flowers. So when Peeta does nothing more than draw a picture of Rue covered with flowers during his skill evaluation before the Quarter Quell, he shocks people with his audacity. When asked why he did it, he replies, "I just wanted to hold them accountable, if only for a moment . . . for killing that little girl."[25] Of course, that sort of thinking is forbidden, and Peeta is warned that the Capitol will try to punish him for such an act of rebellion.

The last thing oppressors can permit is to be reminded of and therefore held accountable for their actions. Even acknowledging the actions of their predecessors, which gained them the lives of privilege and power they now enjoy, is too potentially damaging. This is why history is written by the victors. The true stories of those they defeated or oppressed, and of their own less than honorable actions in doing so, are too dangerous to be told.

This tendency was painfully illustrated in 2010 in my home state of Texas when the Board of Education voted to revise Texas history books. These revisions deliberately left out references to the slaughter of Native Americans and Hispanics during the era of U.S. expansionism, as well as any mention of the Ku Klux Klan. In these new textbooks, the Civil Rights era is barely mentioned and the accomplishments of many women, Hispanic, and African-American scientists, economists, and artists have also been eliminated, ignoring their struggle in overcoming oppression. There was even an attempt to rebrand the African slave trade as "Atlantic triangular trade" which emphasized the economic development of America as opposed to the injustice of slavery that development relied upon. Public outcry stopped that particular change from being passed, but in the end the resulting textbooks presented a version of history where the United States has never done wrong.[26] The stories of pain that shaped the lives of thousands were silenced.

Hiding those ugly parts of history does a disservice to those upon whom the injustices of the past were inflicted—hindering their ability to mourn. It also hurts those who are denied the opportunity to repent of their complicity in the oppression of others—whether through past involvement or from reaping the ongoing benefits.

This is a reality that Germany knows all too well. While there is no denying the horrors and atrocities of the Holocaust, Germany knows that the only honest way to deal with the sins of its past is to never forget them. After the War, the watching world wouldn't allow them a perfunctory policy of forgive and forget when faced with their country's attempt to eradicate an entire ethnic group. Instead, Jewish families were given reparations and memorials were built to ensure that the deaths of millions of Jews, Gypsies, and gays and lesbians could never be forgotten. Even more than sixty years later, the German Chancellor, knowing apologies weren't enough, admitted to Germany's great shame and bowed before the victims of the Holocaust.[27] The former Israeli ambassador to Germany, Avi Primor, once mused: "Where in the world has one ever seen a nation that erects memorials to immortalize its own shame? Only the Germans had the bravery and the humility."[28] Of course, memorials will never be enough to fully atone for such extreme acts of oppression, but Germany knew that it had to do something to make even the smallest steps of healing possible. They are not trying to eliminate the Holocaust from their textbooks or revise history to make themselves appear guiltless. It is an act of bravery and humility to admit one's own shame— to speak of one's sins and accept responsibility for them.

Sadly, in the United States, the sins of our national past have not always been treated as bravely. For example, in 1970 for the annual reenactment of the first Thanksgiving at Plymouth Rock—a festive tourist attraction complete with costumes, prayers, and parade—the organizers wanted to highlight the relations between the Pilgrims and the Wampanoag tribe since that year marked the 350th anniversary of the Pilgrims' arrival. To do so, the organizers invited the current leader of the Wampanoag, Frank James, to deliver a speech for the occasion. James wrote his speech based on the Pilgrims' own recorded account of their first year in the area, which included how they had opened Native graves in search of treasure, forcefully took food from Native tribes, and then captured and sold Native Americans as slaves. Although his speech told such truths as part of the process of reconciliation, the organizers rejected it for being too inflammatory. The truth about history was rejected by those not brave enough to face it. Rejected from the official Thanksgiving celebration, James instead delivered his speech on a nearby hill, thereby establishing the first National Day of Mourning. Every year since a group has gathered there for a National Day of Mourning, committing to gather as long as there are injustices in our nation that need to be mourned. At times, the gathering has been met with armed police and state troopers, but since 1998 it has been permitted to assemble—as long as it doesn't interfere in any way with the official Thanksgiving celebration.[29]

Ignorance and denial of cultural sins can cause tremendous pain to others, but it is even worse when those sins are celebrated and cherished. I've heard people defend the enslavement of Africans as being an improvement in their lives, or justified by their ultimate conversion to Christianity. As they see it, being stripped of all freedoms, separated from family, and abused regularly by masters who nevertheless housed, clothed, and introduced slaves to Christianity was far better than allowing the Africans to remain in their "pagan" tribes. Same story with Native Americans. Some actually defend the genocide, broken promises, and confinement to reservations as a miracle since it eliminated any "demonic" opposition to the spread of "Christian" culture in the United States. I wish I could say I'm making this stuff up, but this defense and celebration of the pain and suffering of others is all too common—even in the church, thereby hindering the tangible realization of the Kingdom of God in our midst.

We Have So Little Communication with Anyone Outside Our District

Richard Twiss, a Christian communicator and member of the Lakota Sioux tribe, knows that it is only through confession—the act of mourning one's sin by literally telling the story of that sin to another—that people can be made whole. He has written about the problems that develop when white Christians make no effort to understand the pain of Native peoples and instead believe the injustices of history were somehow part of God's will. Such a stance not only perpetuates the suffering of Native peoples, it also prevents the fruits of the Spirit—love, joy, peace, etc.—from flourishing among those who support such injustice. On the other hand, Twiss has witnessed how "When Anglo brethren have stood before their Native brethren and honestly, humbly and corporately confessed their neglect and rejection of them and then have spoken of how much they need them, the Holy Spirit has consistently released floods of forgiveness and healing."[30]

Only when that process of confession and repentance is respected and allowed to unfold are people able to move forward in their journey to find healing, comfort, and wholeness. Those who caused the pain must take the time to understand and empathize with the suffering, must offer their confession for past injustices. And for that to happen, people must first get to know one another.

When Katniss teams up with Rue during her first Hunger Games, they spend a good deal of time talking about their respective districts. Rue tells of the harshness of the oppression in District 11 and Katniss is shocked to learn how much worse it is there than even in District 12. Katniss acknowledges that the Gamemakers are most likely blocking their conversation on the broadcast of the Games because the Capitol does not want for the districts to know about one another.

Hearing the plight of others can help the mourning process begin. Just as it is vital to remember the stories of those one has lost, so is learning the stories of others as well. Knowing that one's story has been heard—that the ravages of injustice will not recur simply because they have been forgotten—brings comfort to the suffering. Having others care enough to learn your story, to hear about your pain, is a reminder that you are not alone, but are instead part of a larger family that loves enough to help each other through the mourning process.

It was the way of the Roman Empire, as with the Capitol, to not care enough about those stories to let them be known. Bible scholar Walter Brueggemann summed it up well when he wrote, "Empires do not grieve, do not notice human suffering, do not acknowledge torn bodies or abused villages."[31] Letting those stories be known would get in the way of an empire's ability to use people for its own ends. So their policy is to not notice, not care.

This is why Jesus's habit of noticing the suffering and the outcasts and taking the time to hear their stories presented such a radically alternative way to live. When his disciples tried to shoo children away, Jesus welcomed the children with open arms. When a bleeding (and therefore ritually unclean) woman approached Jesus for healing, he did not shun her but healed her and called her blessed. When a woman broke through the constraints placed on her gender and sat at the feet of a wandering rabbi, Jesus told her indignant sister that she was welcome. And when at a well Jesus encountered a woman from a different ethnic group whose culture shunned her for losing her "honor," Jesus subverted expectations by engaging her in conversation and commissioning her as the first evangelist.

Jesus showed that living in the Kingdom of God means welcoming those who face oppression and suffering and being close enough to learn their stories so we can empathize as they mourn. But as Jesus demonstrated, this might mean challenging cultural constraints and seeing things that those in power might not want us to notice. And it might mean finally listening to stories that reveal our own complicity in oppression and injustice.

Unlike those who try to rewrite or remove the embarrassing stories of our past from history textbooks or silence them at our gatherings, those that live in the way of the Kingdom of God know they must be brave enough and humble enough to let those stories enter into our communal mourning process. This is what South Africa realized after the end of Apartheid. While they realized that punishing everyone who had contributed to the injustice of that system would destroy the country and make truth even harder to uncover, they also knew that it would further victimize people if their stories of oppression were not publically acknowledged. Their solution was to grant amnesty to anyone willing to take responsibility for their actions by making a full and public confession. The Truth and Reconciliation Committee headed by former Anglican Archbishop Desmond Tutu knew that not everyone would be satisfied with this process, but that telling the truth about the years of oppression was a vital part of the mourning process that could bring healing to their broken country.[32]

In the United States, a similar process of mourning might mean telling and listening to the stories of the slaughter and cultural oppression of Native Americans and Mexicans who suffered because someone else wanted the land they called home. It means making space for the stories of those whose enslavement and subsequent denial of decent education, jobs, and rights bolstered economic systems that many of us still benefit from today. It means listening to the stories of the people whose farming and fishing lands have been destroyed by pollution from unregulated factories and refineries. It means listening to the stories of the people who labor long hours to grow our produce and yet can barely afford to feed their families. It means listening to the stories of the women who sew our clothes while facing daily abuse and substandard wages.

In our wired world, where such information is readily available at the click of a mouse, surprisingly few people take the time to listen. Some deny that such stories exist, some insist that such stories have nothing to do with them, some say they find those stories too disturbing to listen to, and some dismiss them, saying there is nothing we can do about them anyway. But when we deny, disassociate, dismiss, or simply refuse to listen to such stories we permit their oppression to continue.

Remembering such stories and taking responsibility for communal sins is something we see repeatedly in the Old Testament scriptures. Leaders like Nehemiah and Daniel spend time in prayer confessing to the communal sins of Israel. They understand that their identity as individuals derives from their connection to community, and thus even the sins of generations past are their responsibility. In accepting inclusion in the community of God's people, they intuitively know that healing the effects of past injustices within that corporate body is an important part of what it means to belong.

Sadly, that sense of communal responsibility has been lost for many North American Christians. Many not only avoid examining and confessing corporate and national sins, but insist that past and current injustices have absolutely nothing to do with them. Unlike the communal culture that shaped Jesus's message, modern American culture has bought into the false message that it is possible to be an isolated individual whose responsibility is only to oneself. As Christian professor and author Soong-Chan Rah writes, "Corporate sin is so disconnected from the reality of our typical American Christian life that we are shocked when it actually enters our world. Rather than confront sin, we begin to look for ways to categorize it as a theologically liberal agenda—thereby stripping corporate confession and repentance of its power."[33] If we can label such stories as too liberal, or too guilt inducing, or a distraction from the Bible or theology, or too distant (whether geographically or historically), or simply too hard to deal with—it becomes much easier to avoid any sense of responsibility.

But the reality is that we do live in community—and this, in our current age, is a global community. Our isolationist excuses can't negate that connectedness. The choices we make on a daily basis—what to buy, where to live, who to be friends with, who to vote for, how to give of our time and energy, etc.—have an impact on the ongoing realities of violence, exploitation, and oppression in our world. And even when the original injustices are now long in the past (as with slavery or the Native American genocide, for instance), those living today continue to reap the benefits or negative after-effects of these past events. (How many of us here in North America, for example, do not live on land that at some point was violently taken from its original inhabitants?) We are more connected to our ancestors than we realize, and continue to bear a responsibility for righting their wrongs.

Confession and repentance are necessarily difficult. But being in conversation with the oppressed, especially those we or our ancestors have had a role in oppressing, shouldn't be avoided simply because it's hard. Not if we claim to care about living in the way of the Kingdom of God. The difficult process of mourning is a prerequisite for receiving comfort.

A friend from New Zealand with whom I attended seminary once laughed at us Americans in class one day when a number of fellow students asserted that we needn't bother worrying about the slaughter of the Native Americans because doing anything about it now would just be too difficult. He pointed out that in New Zealand, where the once oppressed indigenous Maori population still makes up around 15 percent of the population, they have had no choice but to engage in the difficult (and ongoing) process of communal mourning and reconciliation. In the United States, where Native Americans represent barely 1 percent of the national population, it is easier to ignore their story and avoid working for reconciliation. But as much as we would like to pretend that we are not communal beings still connected to such past events, that is not the way of Jesus, nor should it be the way of those who claim to follow him. Instead, the church has the difficult but blessed opportunity to help the world mourn and heal.

I Have To at Least Try

As followers of Christ, we need to go out of our way to listen to the stories of the oppressed. But we also need to discover how our lifestyle choices contribute to oppression in the world today. We need to know the stories of the people who grow our food, sew our clothes, assemble our electronics, mine our coal, and wash our dishes. Are we contributing to their oppression or are we helping them be comforted? We need to know our country's true history and be honest about how its success and economic strength has been built upon a long list of injustices. We need to be aware of how many of the benefits we take for granted today are often rooted in the slaughter of Natives, the seizure of other's lands, and the enslavement of Africans. We need to hear such truths not so that we can simply feel guilty or bad about ourselves, but so that the reconciliation and repentance that mark the Kingdom of God can flourish.

Hearing those stories is the first step in the mourning process. The next step involves repentance—a word that literally means to stop in our tracks, turn around, and choose a different way. It means being brave enough to apologize. Humble enough to try to make amends. And loving enough to accept how difficult that path will be. Like Germany discovered after the Holocaust, there can never be enough apologies, but they still must occur if true mourning is to take place.

But it doesn't stop there. Being with those who mourn changes us. It isn't enough to just be aware of the problems and feel sorry about them, although that's where those of us unused to mourning must begin. Entering into relationship can lead to true reconciliation. Those once involved in oppression come to know those they have hurt; and it is very difficult to continue harming a person while helping him to mourn his pain at the same time. We then become motivated to end our involvement in economic, political, and social injustice. But this will require us to sacrifice our need for control or to always be right and instead respect those we are in relationship with enough to learn from them. In loving others enough to make their mourning, healing, and comfort possible, we miraculously discover the same blessing for ourselves.

When Katniss tries to comfort the injured and dying Rue in the Games, Rue asks Katniss to sing for her. Singing is something that Katniss hasn't allowed herself to do much since her father's death, but music is Rue's favorite thing in the world. Katniss, fatigued and emotionally exhausted, realizes that if this is Rue's final request, she has "to at least try."[34] So to comfort the girl who, against the Capitol's desires, she had truly gotten to know and care for, Katniss sings to Rue as she dies. It is an act of forbidden mourning that not only helps Rue die with the knowledge that someone cares for her, but helps Katniss reconnect to a part of herself that she had suppressed. By mourning with Rue, she too, if only for a brief moment, experiences some of the blessings that come from mourning.

The Kingdom of God is a place of mourning. Even if it means subverting the mandates of the powers that be, following the way of Jesus means that we never pretend all is well when all is obviously not well. Living into the Kingdom of God means allowing pain and suffering to be healed. It means committing to the hard path of mourning even if it is embarrassing or involves repentance and sacrifice. For as Jesus promised, and Katniss discovered, those who are able to mourn are blessed because the process of mourning brings its own comfort.

Chapter Three
The Meek: Supporting One Body, Many Districts

"Blessed are the meek, for they will inherit the earth."
~ Matthew 5:5

Volunteers Are All but Extinct

When Katniss hears her sister's name called at the Reaping her first reaction is utter shock. She just stands there unable to breathe or speak, utterly stunned. But as soon as she sees her pale, resolute sister walking toward the stage, Katniss rushes forward, pushes her sister behind her, and volunteers to take her place. At first no one knows how to handle the situation, for while any other child could volunteer to take someone else's place (and in some Districts people are actually trained to do so) in District 12 where "the word *tribute* is pretty much synonymous with the word *corpse*, volunteers are all but extinct."[35] But Katniss doesn't volunteer for the dubious glory of a chance to win the games; she lays down her life because she loves her sister and wants to protect her. In short, she exhibits a spirit of meekness.

The idea of meekness has gotten a bad rap in our culture. Maybe that is because it rhymes with "weakness," but it is often confused with extreme mousiness, social awkwardness, and a tendency to let people walk all over you. Even Jesus's statement, "blessed are the meek," is often reduced to nothing more than a patronizing expression of pity for those lacking the wherewithal to do something with their lives. But to be meek has nothing to do with being weak. While in modern English we associate the term with weakness, the Greek term used in the Bible, *praus*, connotes strength under control. It implies a person's ability to control their impulses and desires so as to love and serve others around them. The meek are gentle and kind not because others dominate them into submission, but because they choose to devote themselves to others. The meek don't let others walk all over them, but they do often willingly give up something for the sake of someone else. Be that a desire for power, the need to be right, a sense of entitlement, or even one's own security, the meek willingly lay aside such things for the benefit of the greater good. As others have described it, meekness is about "replacing the clenched fist of self-protection with an open hand of welcome and service."[36]

Like Katniss volunteering to take her sister's place in the Hunger Games, the meek willingly and deliberately make their choices oriented around the love and service of others. They aren't bullied into giving up a part of themselves; it is part of their core identity to live in such a self-sacrificial way. And though not quite as extinct as volunteering as tribute in District 12, living a life characterized by meekness is still rare in our world today.

It is easy to understand why. Our world isn't organized around the idea of sacrificial living. In the United States especially, we have been conditioned to prize the idea of the rugged individualist living the American Dream—where our personal pursuit of happiness is often far more important than life and liberty for all. Living that dream is all about building our own personal empires of wealth, success, and happiness. A constant barrage of commercials tell us "Buy this Product to be Happy or Successful or Attractive," but what they don't even need to sell us on is that our personal happiness should always be our main concern—that's a given in our culture. While the occasional heroic act of sacrifice might be applauded, the very fact that we honor such actions reveals that they are not the norm. Let's face it, looking out for number one, prattling on about our entitlements, and complaining when having to accommodate the needs of others are far more common behaviors. There is a place for healthy self-care and enjoyment of life, but the tendency in our world is to place our own comforts and needs before those of others. It's harsh, but sadly true.

Just as the Citizens of the Capitol of Panem responded to the drastic food shortages and evacuations caused by the rebellion by hoarding all that they could find and locking their doors to the suddenly homeless, our own first instinct is often to protect what we assume is ours by right. From complaining about our hard-earned wages being taxed to fund schools and roads to saying it is much too difficult to take the time to care for the environment or to shop ethically, the inconvenience of making even the smallest sacrifices for others is too much for some of us. We often respond to calls for sacrificial living like the teenager I once worked with, who responded to hearing about how much of our clothing has ties to unjust sweatshop practices with, "You're asking me to change how I *shop*? Like that's ever going to happen!" Such a call is hard because it goes against our culture's message that a successful life means having (and keeping) it all. Even some churches preach that material blessing (the more ostentatious the better) is a sure sign of God's favor.

But Jesus talked about blessings a bit differently. He said, "Blessed are the meek, for they will inherit the earth" (Mt. 5:5). In a world where material wealth and worldly power define the highest goals of many, Jesus subversively claimed that the meek are blessed because they are the true "rulers" of the earth. The ones who willingly give up power and privilege for the sake of others are the ones who are deemed blessed in the world where God's dreams are realized. Understanding that all of the earth is the Lord's, they know that any blessing in their lives is there to share with others. Such meekness acknowledges God's sovereignty over all things, admitting that God's ways are better than the tight-fisted ways of the world.

At the same time, living meekly is vastly different than simply letting others walk all over you. While those under oppression, like the people Jesus usually addressed, could certainly embody meekness, it is not the slave morality that some have dismissed it as. To willingly suffer injustice and the denial of all one's freedoms and rights is not to live in a way that cares for the well-being of all. When people around you are being hurt, risking your safety to help protect them is a display of meekness. Many oppressors have kept people subjugated by insisting they display a false version of the "Christian" virtue of meekness as fearful compliance, and yet this is not what meekness actually signifies in scripture. Instead, true meekness serves others by working to end injustice.

The meek take seriously the idea that we exist in the Kingdom of God as part of the body of Christ. Those created in the image of God are part of this body, our brothers and sisters as fellow children of God. And as Paul writes, "If one member suffers, all suffer together with it" (1 Cor. 12:26). One member of the body cannot say to another "I have no need of you," or "my needs are more important than yours." Those that do not see themselves as mere individuals looking out for number one, but as members of this interconnected body, live in ways that care for the health of that body. They acknowledge that we are all created in the image of God. This means, as Desmond Tutu wrote, that "each one of us is a God-carrier, God's viceroy, God's representative. It is because of this fact that to treat one such person as if he or she were less than this is veritably blasphemous. It is spitting in the face of God."[37] The meek therefore love the fellow image-bearers to the extent that they are willing to make personal sacrifices for the sake of love. It may be true that people who live this way are nearly as extinct as tribute volunteers were in District 12, but this is the way of life God has called the citizens of his Kingdom to live.

Aren't They the Very Reason I Have to Fight?

Paul's imagery of the body was no arbitrary metaphor. He specifically designed it to challenge Stoic philosophy's "fable of the body" that held influence in the Roman Empire.[38] While many of the elements in the Stoic version of the metaphor are the same as Paul's, they differ significantly in purpose. The Roman elite used this tale of many people making up one functioning body to justify their positions of wealth and power. They wielded the fable like a weapon, using it to scare the plebeians into submission. Slaves and oppressed workers were threatened that the entire body could collapse if they failed to do their job or if they caused any sort of unrest. To the powerful Romans, the image of "one body, many parts" was a means of imposing order and making sure everyone stayed in their rightful place. There were the privileged rulers and the lowly workers; it was obvious which parts of the body were more important than others.

But in the upside-down way of the Kingdom of God, Paul takes this tale of oppression and turns it into a message of hope. He writes that, yes, in Christ we are one body with many parts, each bearing different gifts, but that being part of a body should lead us to "be devoted to one another in love. Honor one another above yourselves" (Rom. 12:10 TNIV). Instead of a means for clinging to power through the subjugation of others, being members of one body levels the playing field. All parts of the body are necessary and are to be honored and treated with affection. Being part of the body of Christ is not about striving to be on top or grasp the American Dream at any cost, but about meekly presenting oneself as a living sacrifice in service to others. Unlike the Empire, which is intent on manipulating the many parts of its body, the body of Christ offers a way to be in community that respects the dignity of all God's children.

The strength of this image of a communal body is what enables the powerful to use it to manipulate and suppress others. Indeed, President Snow uses a similar argument to threaten Katniss into doing his will. After she outsmarts the Hunger Games by finding a way for both her and Peeta to survive, an act perceived as defiance against the Capitol, President Snow pays her a chilling visit. He not only threatens to harm all those she loves if she doesn't do everything in her power to discourage rebellion, he also places the well-being and survival of the entire country on her shoulders. He tells her that a rebellion would destroy the country and that if the Capitol released its control on the districts the entire system would collapse resulting in countless deaths.

Given his cruel history of oppressing the districts and forcing them to send their children to die as tributes in the Games, it is obvious Snow couldn't care less about the people of Panem. He simply wants to preserve the position of power he ruthlessly fought to obtain. Nevertheless, he understands that Katniss thinks more communally. From volunteering to take her sister's place in the Games to teaming up with the youngest and weakest player to putting herself in danger in order to keep Peeta alive, Katniss lives out the way of meekness and compassion that Paul uses to describe the true communal body ethic. Snow grasps this and tries to use it to keep her under his control. He tells her, "Katniss Everdeen, the girl who was on fire, you have provided a spark that, left unattended, may grow to an inferno that destroys Panem."[39] And Katniss, who does care more for others than herself, responds exactly as he thought she would, saying that she will do whatever he tells her to do.

Katniss has to realize that Panem is already destroyed before she dares question the absolute authority of President Snow. A country suffering under conditions of dire poverty and extreme oppression is not a healthy functioning body. Telling the suffering masses that everything will fall apart if they step out of line is nothing but a calculated lie on the part of the powerful. Everything has already fallen apart for everyone except the privileged and powerful few. But it is not until Katniss's friend Gale questions her decision to help protect President Snow's status quo that she begins to see things differently. Challenging her assumption that the people are safe, he asks her how safe it is to have to work like slaves, live on the brink of starvation, and have their children put up for the Reaping. When people are oppressed they are not safe. To see each other as honored members of the same body means caring about each other's well-being, and, as Paul wrote, loving them and honoring their needs above one's own. Or, to quote Joss Whedon's infamous Dr. Horrible, the point is "destroying the status quo because the status is *not* quo."[40]

This is what the meek do—care for others. Unlike those who are only concerned with protecting and promoting their own interests, the meek truly work for the good of the communal body. Once Katniss understands that protecting an oppressive status quo was not the best way to care for the people of Panem, she realizes that she must strive to help everyone live in a better world. Thinking of those who had been hurt, she realizes, "Prim . . . Rue . . . aren't they the very reason I have to fight? Because what has been done to them is so wrong, so beyond justification, so evil that there is no choice?"[41] Her own interests and even safety are secondary to her commitment to end oppression and injustice so the entire body can be healthy and whole.

But, as Jesus revealed in his Parable of the Talents, what one is forced to endure in choosing to care for the whole body instead of merely shoring up the privilege and power of the few, can be costly. The parable tells of a harsh ruler who traveled to a foreign land to secure his position from the emperor while a delegation from his own country followed to request that this oppressive man not be permitted to rule. Scholars have pointed out that this "opening scene is a thinly veiled retelling of Herod Archelaus's embassy to Rome in 4 B.C.E. to seek imperial confirmation of his authority" complete with the accompanying Jewish protest of his rule—an event with which Jesus's listeners would have been very familiar.[42] As he left, the ruler entrusted a few of his slaves with some money and commanded them to do business while he was away. Upon returning, with his power to rule secured despite the local opposition, he demanded an accounting of their business. Two slaves had managed to gain significant profits from the money. In Jesus's day, such a large return on investment could only have been possible "through gross exploitation of the poor"—perhaps by charging extreme interest rates (a practice forbidden by Jewish law) on loans offered to the desperately poor.[43] One slave, however, refused to participate in these exploitative financial practices and simply returned the money to the ruler, naming the ruler's sins in the process. The slave says to him "you are a harsh man; you take what you did not deposit, and reap what you did not sow" (Lk. 19:21). In response, the ruler not only rewards those who increased his wealth through whatever means necessary, but strips the other slave of the little he already had and ordered the slaughter of all those who protested his appointment. The ruler's oppressive and manipulative stance is summed up in his statement: "I tell you, to all those who have, more will be given; but from those who have nothing, even what they have will be taken away" (Lk. 19:26). Like President Snow oppressing the Districts of Panem in order to increase his wealth and power, the ruler in Jesus's parable cares little for the actual needs of the people.

It is a harsh story, but the writer of Luke mentions that Jesus told it because some of his followers "supposed that the Kingdom of God was to appear immediately" (Lk. 19:11). Jesus needed to make sure they understood that living in the Kingdom is something that doesn't just happen overnight but is instead a long and often difficult process. The slave in the parable that meekly put others first and lived out the lifestyle Jesus modeled didn't change the world and bring about the Kingdom in its fullness with his one action. The oppressive ruler didn't give up power or stop his unjust acts; instead he punished those who tried to take a stand for justice. The world doesn't take kindly to those who challenge what it holds dear. To live meekly is to remember the people for whom we are making our sacrifices at those times when the world punishes us for caring about the whole body more than ourselves. The meek do inherit the earth, but the journey there is a long and arduous one.

This Is the Sort of Future a Rebellion Could Bring

While Jesus's parable warns against assuming that acts of meekness could ever transform the world immediately, there are moments of hope where the meek get glimpses of the sort of world their sacrifices are working to create. We see this when Katniss gets a chance to chat with her sister Prim during the rebellion. Having been evacuated from District 12 where she often didn't know if there would be enough to eat each day, Prim is thriving physically and mentally in District 13. Her skills as a healer are recognized and she is given the opportunity to train as a doctor. Even amidst the despair of war, Katniss realizes that this is something Prim could never have dreamed of before. For the first time, the spark of hope kindles within Katniss as she realizes that "this is the sort of future a rebellion could bring."[44] She finally glimpses a tangible outcome from all the sacrifices that before had seemed insignificant next to the vast injustices of her world.

These small glimpses of hope make it easier to grasp how to live as a communal body in our globalized world. While we can easily see how sacrifices we make for our own families benefit them, it is often hard to wrap our minds around living sacrificially for strangers. Facts and statistics can show the global impact of giving to global aid causes, shopping ethically, or living more environmentally-friendly, but numbers aren't always the best motivators—especially when the siren call of culture is trying to convince us not to care. Stories of individual lives changed are what really remind us that there is hope and that orienting our lives around the way of love for the long haul makes a difference for the Kingdom.

Of course, unlike Prim, most children in the Districts who grew up malnourished and with no educational opportunities have little hope of ever achieving a better life. If they survive to adulthood, there is little they can do but offer their own children more of the same. A similar thing happens psychologically to children who are never encouraged to care for others or live sacrificially. If one was never exposed as a child to the hope living meekly can bring to the world, it becomes even harder to live this way as an adult, and harder still if one was insulated from the very reasons why this world needs hope.

As Katniss discovers, citizens of the Capitol are so unaware of conditions in the districts that it is nearly impossible for them to empathize with the suffering there, much less make sacrifices on their behalf. Even with Katniss, who had just survived the arena, her prep team can only talk about the Games in reference to themselves. They chatter on about the very things Katniss would rather forget, but their talk is only about what they were doing or how they felt when a specific event in the Games occurred.

Meekness is a deliberate choice, but it is one that emerges out of who we were shaped to be. Children who are taught to see the needs of others, to care for the well-being of all, and to share willingly with others have a far stronger ability to continue living in ways that bring hope and love to the world. It is like that famous saying, "The battle of Waterloo was won on the playing fields of Eton." Lives of service and love don't just emerge in the moment of crisis; we exhibit such things because we were formed in the way of service and love (the soldiers at Waterloo learned how to be disciplined in school at Eton). Kind and caring people were taught to value such things and therefore can more easily live in such ways.

Sadly however, there are elements in our culture today that try to restrict the ability of children to learn about living as part of a body. Extreme examples of this are the "Vacation Liberty Schools" that Tea Party-influenced churches launched in 2010, described as "Vacation Bible Schools—Glenn Beck style."[45] The curriculum includes a game where children must use water pistols to shoot soap bubbles out of the air. The objective is to realize that they can do a much better job if they have their own bucket from which to refill their guns, instead of needing to share a communal bucket with others. While I can understand a desire to subtly warn children about the dangers of totalitarian Communism, it is hard not to find games that encourage kids not to share a bit disturbing.

But even if such events are an extreme, I have also noticed recent trends among parents who seem to be raising kids to care more about looking out for number one than about caring for others around them. I see it when I take my kids to the pool and, even as I am instructing my 3-year-old on needing to wait his turn for the slide, I see parents actually shoving other kids out of the way so their kids can cut to the front of the line. I see it when parents label, mock, and dismiss as "politically correct" efforts to teach their children to use polite language that does not hurt or demean others. I hear it from the suburban middle school teachers who tried to start a food and clothing drive for the homeless, but received complaints from parents who thought it might be too mentally disturbing for their children to discover that homeless people exist.

And I saw it when my husband and I were serving as church youth ministers and invited teens to participate in World Vision's 30 Hour Famine—a program where students fast for thirty hours to show solidarity with and raise money for the global poor. Though the fasting was noncompulsory, we still had a number of parents upset that we would dare ask their kids go a day without eating. When we tried to explain that fasting was a spiritual discipline and that to go one day without a meal was just a small way to begin understanding and empathizing with the kind of hunger much of the world faces every day, we were informed that those people obviously didn't have to deal with the rigors of high school. We didn't push the issue with those parents—how they raised their children was their decision—but it was sobering to hear them discourage their kids from empathizing with those in need.

Of course, not all children are encouraged to care only about themselves, but it seems to be a rising trend, especially among the middle and upper classes in the United States. Unlike Katniss, who took the time to care for others even while desperately trying to survive herself, more privileged American children often miss out on the opportunity to live the blessed life of meekness. Overly sheltering children from the harsh realities of the world has also kept them from developing the spiritual ability to love their neighbor. Ironically (or predictably, depending on your level of cynicism), The Hunger Games series has become one more thing parents are trying to protect their children from. In 2011, the American Library Association's annual top 10 list of books most criticized in their communities placed The Hunger Games at number five.[46] As a book about oppression and war, it is not surprising that parents complained about the violence in the books. Surprisingly, however, the challenges to the books came from middle and high schools. The series was obviously not intended for young children, but directed at the same age group that faces Reaping for the Hunger Games in the books: 12- to 18-year-olds. But, as one mother of a middle-school student in New Hampshire complained, reading The Hunger Games could encourage students to be entertained by the murdering of other children and lead to another Columbine-like school shooting.

One of course wonders if that mother had even read the book or simply missed the entire point the book makes about the awfulness of being entertained by violence and insensitive to the suffering of others. However, the assumption that teenagers should not be encouraged to think critically about real issues in the world is what I find most unsettling. Well-written fiction presents the reader with opportunities to make choices about the world and to interrogate his or her own society. Books are safe places to practice the art of being in relationship with others vastly different from oneself, to discover that we are all connected and therefore have obligations to one another. To care for and stand in solidarity with the suffering, one must first be aware that violence and oppression exist in the world. It is hard to see oneself as part of a body if one is kept ignorant about the very existence of other body parts.

Sheltering teenagers from harsh realities does them a disservice not only by making them ill prepared when they actually do encounter such things, but also by encouraging them to assume their own comfort and ease is far more important than the well-being of others. The world is full of people who look after only their own interests. As Katniss discovers in dealing with President Snow and President Coin, there are people who will do anything to be powerful, even if that means hurting others in the process. When life is all about me, it is easy to become apathetic about the suffering of others. With this mindset it doesn't matter if my consumer choices are contributing to workers being abused or exploited. It doesn't matter if my daily habits harm the environment and contribute to the destruction of people's homes. It doesn't matter if people of a different skin color or gender are marginalized so long as I get ahead. Growing up without being required to think about the plight of others can create adults who have neither the means to understand how their choices affect other people, nor any reason to care. It produces adults who believe the world is there for the taking, and not the meek members of the body of Christ who are concerned with the health of the whole.

But despite efforts to prevent teenagers from being exposed to the harsh realities of our world, even the most sheltered of students reading The Hunger Games have nevertheless grown up in the violence of a post-9/11 globalized world. For most young people, a world where the United States is at war and where we live under the constant threat of terror is the only world they can consciously remember. Just as Katniss must be told after the war begins, "There's no going back. So we might as well get on with things," we too must accept that we live in a different world.[47] The world is full of violence and societal systems that treat human beings as tools to be used instead of people to be loved. One can respond with more violence, or one can choose to live as part of the body of Christ.

The meek choose the way of love. Imposing oneself over and above others through physical, legal, economic, or religious violence is the opposite of existing meekly as part of a healthy and whole body. Using "safe" stories like The Hunger Games to help young people think through the full cost of the violence they will inevitably encounter and be forced to choose to participate in or not is part of healthy moral formation that shapes them into the sort of people they will be in the world. That is the power of a good story, it teaches us about ourselves and how to be better people living in a community.

I Want Her on My Team

The meek will inherit the earth because they possess a special sort of power. It is not the sort of power that places one above others, but the sort that helps guide people into a better world. Caring enough about others to make sacrifices in one's own life may be rare. But, when it does happen, it inspires people, giving them hope—which is of course why it scares those who cling to the domineering sort of power. It comes as a surprise to Katniss, after visiting a hospital to comfort the wounded and dying, when she realizes why so many people want to use her for their own purposes. People look up to her; she inspires them to have hope. She realizes that "I have a kind of power I never knew I possessed."[48] She realizes that President Snow knew this and tried to use it for his own ends, as did the rebel leader Plutarch and District 13's President Coin. In contrast, Katniss's own natural instinct was to help others and put their interests ahead of her own. That sort of sacrificial love is contagious and inspiring. Katniss became a symbol of hope just by being her naturally meek self. It took her time to realize her own power, and that possessing it meant those who cared about having power would either attempt to use her or destroy her. But once she did, she chose to use that power for better ends, to love and serve others.

All along Katniss had been wary of those with the power to manipulate and control others. While some thought the smartest strategy in the Games would be to align with the strongest players, Katniss wanted nothing to do with those who eagerly sought to win through violence at any cost. In her first games she aligned with the youngest player, Rue, and the wounded Peeta. When she returned for the Quarter Quell games it was the tributes who demonstrated meekness that she gravitated toward—people like Mags, the elderly woman who volunteered to take the place of Annie, a champion whose first trip to the Games had left her mentally unstable. As a strategy for winning the Games, teaming up with an elderly woman made no sense, but as someone who cared more about community than power, Katniss decided, "I want her on my team."[49]

This is the sort of community that is formed when meekness guides our actions. A community where all members—old, young, suffering, or healthy—are included and cared for. In opposition to the ways of the world in which other people are simply things to be used by those in positions of privilege and power, the meek realize that we have no choice but to exist as parts of one body. We can either live only for ourselves at the expense of the rest of the body, or we can embrace our identity as part of that whole. Living as part of the body is difficult and requires sacrifice, which is why it is the meek who will inherit the earth. They are the ones who are best prepared to live in ways that create a healthy and functioning body where all the parts are cherished, and they have the power to inspire others to do the same.

That is how and why the meek are blessed. They are blessed by that experience of true community. They don't strive to make it their own, fearful that at any point they might lose a bit of their treasured position or possessions. Instead, they live as one humble part of the whole body, seeking to make a better world for all—making real the Kingdom of God.

If we too, like Katniss, desire to be part of this blessed community, we must lay down our selfishness and fear and choose to embrace meekness.

Chapter Four
Those Who Hunger and Thirst for Righteousness: Loving Like the Boy with the Bread

"Blessed are those who hunger and thirst for righteousness, for they will be filled."
~ Matthew 5:6

I Don't Want Them to Change Me in There

The system of bread and circus thrives in Panem because of the Hunger Games. The people in the Districts hunger both for actual bread to fill their starving bellies and for freedom from the oppressive control of the Capitol. The citizens of the Capitol hunger to be entertained, to be distracted and thrilled with the latest gossip, fashions, and sick human drama of the Games. The leaders of Panem hunger too—for power and control over the masses who toil to fill their insatiable desires. The Hunger Games continue because some desires can never be satisfied. Hunger that allows some to live in luxury while others starve does not ultimately fulfill. The hunger that devours others—abusing, exploiting, and using them to meet the demands of one's own self-serving appetite—is a hunger that is never filled. It demands more and more, tightening its oppressive grip to extract tribute from those with nothing left to give.

To a people crippled by the demands of the Roman Empire's insatiable appetite, Jesus declared yet another sort of hunger to be blessed. In the Kingdom of God it is not those who devour others through acts of greed and injustice who are blessed, but instead those who hunger and thirst after righteousness, for they shall be filled. Righteousness, which in the Greek is synonymous with (so can also be translated as) *justice*, is a way of living where one participates in the dreams and desires of God. More than simply making right personal choices, righteousness includes working for the *shalom*, or welfare, of the whole community. Living righteously means living rightly in relation to God and others, caring for the needs of others as if they were one's own. Simply put, those who hunger and thirst after righteousness are those who desire to see the Kingdom of God manifest on earth as in heaven.

Unlike those who hunger after that which the world values—power, wealth, possessions—and pursue them through acts of unrighteousness and oppression, those who hunger after the ways of God can actually be filled. Using others in ways that mock the image of God in them can never bring about the peace and wholeness that can be found in the community of the Kingdom of God. Only by desiring the good of all God's children can one find the fullness and belonging that only God can provide. This is a hunger that builds others up rather than consuming them whole. It gives instead of takes and, according to Jesus, is ultimately most fulfilling.

While the ruling elites in The Hunger Games series make a game of hunger as they manipulate, threaten, and exploit others, we see in the character of Peeta the hunger to always live rightly in the world. While Katniss, growing up as an impoverished child in District 12, had to creatively circumvent the oppressive laws of the Capital in order to help her family and friends survive, Peeta had the luxury of always simply trying to be good. As a middle class baker's son he is one of the few in District 12 who never physically hungers. He is simply a kind person at heart whom others trust because he is always so reliably good. Katniss comes to realize this about him on the train ride to the Capitol after their Reaping. On the train, their mentor Haymitch uses alcohol as a way to escape the horrors of the Games and being forced, year after year, to mentor two children as they are sent to their deaths. After he passes out in his own vomit, Peeta is the one who offers to clean him up and care for him. Seeing that act of compassion pulls Katniss up short. She had assumed that Peeta, like all the other tributes, was automatically her enemy and therefore already at work strategizing ways to beat her. But she realizes that his helping Haymitch has no strategic benefit; it is just part of who Peeta is—a kind and caring person.

Peeta is the sort of person who sees the right thing to do and then tries his best to do it. For instance, on their victory tour after the Hunger Games he and Katniss come face to face with the families of Rue and Thresh, who had both died in the Games. Knowing that an "I'm sorry for your loss" was not enough, Peeta offers their families a month of the winner's wages each year, an amount that can easily provide for a family for a year. He knows he has to do something to help them out, to offer something to heal the pain the Games forced upon them. Instead of merely looking out for his own interests and keeping the wealth for himself, he wants it to bless others, bringing a bit of hope and wholeness to a broken community. For Peeta, striving to live rightly in relation to others is his daily calling.

So when his name is called at the District 12 Reaping, it is not surprising that Katniss notices that his "blue eyes show the alarm I've seen so often in prey."[50] To participate in the fight to the death of the Hunger Games challenges everything that Peeta holds dear. Kindness and compassion have no place in the Capitol's conception of the Games. For one that hungers and thirsts to be a righteous person—to always live rightly in relation to others—a trip to the Games threatens not just his life but the very core of who he is.

The night before they are taken to the Arena, Peeta confesses to Katniss the fear he has of losing his very self: "My best hope is not to disgrace myself and . . . I want to die as myself . . . I don't want them to change me in there. Turn me into some kind of monster that I'm not."[51] He knows what it could cost him to play the part the Capitol wants him to play. To them he is just a pawn, a means of entertaining the citizens of the Capitol and controlling the districts. The desire of one boy to always be good meant little to those who cared only for power at any cost.

The Bread that Gave Me Hope

Striving for righteousness has always been a struggle for those who desire to be in the world but not of it. The way of the world is not to seek the shalom of the community, but to encourage individuals to look out for themselves. This attitude is reflected by the citizens of the Capitol who are obsessed with entertainment and trivialities—the latest fashions and electronics—without bothering to consider the human cost. Their hunger for convenience and pleasure in their day-to-day lives far outweighs any inkling of desire to care for the welfare of the other districts in Panem. When unrest in the districts leads to shortages of luxury goods like electronics and shellfish for the Capitol, the people there don't stop to wonder why the shortages are occurring, they simply complain about the inconvenience to their lives.

A similar situation exists in the Western world today. While some might concern themselves with small scale acts of righteousness—endeavoring to be better parents, or spouses, or employees for the sake of a small handful of other people—it is far rarer to find people who care enough for the entire community, the global community, that they hunger to live in the ways of God's Kingdom.

While Peeta may be afraid the Games will change him from the sacrificially loving person he is at his core, our culture often encourages us not to even bother with such things. But to be in danger of being changed by the culture one first has to be living noticeably different than the culture. As the Catholic Worker Movement holds, we don't live in a society where it is easy for people to be good. All of our culture's incentives encourage us to live for ourselves, not the common good of all. This cultural condition is what prompted the Catholic Worker Movement's founder Dorothy Day to write, "The greatest challenge of the day is: how to bring about a revolution of the heart."[52] Our hearts need to be radically changed before righteousness can be the guiding factor in our lives.

Sadly, even in our churches it can be rare to hear a call to live righteously in ways that put the needs of others before the demands of personal piety. All too often churches are just as consumer-driven and individualistic as the culture around them. Some believe that caring for the welfare of the community must be rejected out of hand as a distraction from the more important demands of personal holiness. In others, while lip service is paid to "loving your neighbor as yourself," the focus typically tends to remain on the second part of that command—ways to love oneself more. Righteousness becomes less about living rightly in relation to God and others and is instead reduced to individual acts of personal piety, or worse, the never-ending consumption of religious goods and services—the latest devotional best-seller, the hottest new worship band, the next big Christian conference or event. Instead of building up the whole community, righteousness gets twisted into a mockery of itself where personal religiosity itself becomes a commodity to be hungered after and consumed. But that is not what Jesus said would bless and fill us.

One finds a poignant example of how the Kingdom of God should instead be transforming the cultural status quo in Jesus's parable of the unforgiving servant (Mt. 18:21-25). In the parable the King forgives the enormous debt of one of his servants—an act of upside-down shalom-affirming economics if there ever was one. But instead of letting the righteous way of the King transform his own life, the servant selfishly hoards the forgiveness for himself. When, shortly thereafter, he encounters another servant who owes him a small debt, he has that man thrown in prison until it is paid back in full. Rather than choosing to act counter-culturally, mercifully, and therefore righteously, the servant desires the blessings of the Kingdom without the hard work of actually living in its ways—what theologian and martyr Dietrich Bonhoeffer called "cheap grace." The servant's actions might have been permissible in the eyes of a cut-throat and self-centered culture, but they failed to establish right relations with not just the King, but the community around him.

When righteousness gets reduced to simply a desire to be individually right with God, one also runs the risk of replacing true righteousness with self-righteousness. Instead of caring about the welfare of all of God's children and hungering to see the dreams of God realized on earth, the self-righteous become consumed with their own spiritual purity. While some, like the unforgiving servant, abandon righteousness for the siren call of culture, the self-righteous are so disgusted by culture that they reject the call to live righteously *within it.* Whether they simply want to avoid sullying themselves with secular politics or culture, or they assume that working against those committing acts of injustice might lead to becoming coercive or violent themselves, the outcome is the same. By focusing on their own purity they fail to work for the shalom of the community.

This is the message the prophet Jeremiah had to deliver to the Israelite exiles living in Babylon. These are the exiles who wondered how they could sing the songs of Zion by the rivers of Babylon (Ps. 137). When their captors asked for them to share the songs of the Lord with them, the exiles hung up their harps, wept, and wished for the heads of the Babylonian babies to be dashed against rocks (as their own had been). They were cut off from their temple and their rituals of purity and thus could not fathom how they could wish anything but ill against their oppressors. As a prophet of God, Jeremiah had to remind them of their identity as people of God. God had chosen the Israelites as a people so that they could in turn bless others (Gen. 12:1-3). Thus, even as Jeremiah encouraged them to mourn and lament, he also reminded them to live righteously in the land of their exile. "Build houses and live in them; plant gardens and eat what they produce . . . seek the welfare of the city where I have sent you into exile, and pray to the Lord on its behalf, for in its welfare you will find your welfare" (Jer. 29:5-7).

Settle down. Plant gardens. Seek the welfare of Babylon. A far cry from their self-righteous, though understandable, calls for revenge. Jeremiah did not hold back in reminding them that God had placed them in Babylon and they needed to stay faithful to the way God called them to live—as righteous people who work for the shalom of all. But living for the sake of others is difficult for those used to managing their own purity as their primary form of worship. It is far easier to take care of oneself than to make sacrifices for the benefit of others. Sadly, the same dynamic Jeremiah had to speak against is still at play in the church today. Many Christians are so disgusted to be in "exile" amidst sinful cultural, economic, and political systems that they metaphorically hang up their harps while cursing and withdrawing from the system. Since the system is evil, they choose to wash their hands of it and refuse to get involved. Their own purity matters more than seeking shalom for all.

While piety and purity are an important part of following God, there are times when solely concentrating on one's individual purity actually enables corporate injustice to flourish. In these situations, caring for the good of the whole body must take precedent. The most famous example of this is Dietrich Bonhoeffer's attempted assassination of Hitler. He didn't just wake up one day and say, "Hey, let's kill Hitler." He fully acknowledged that an act of murder was wrong, but after long deliberation he knew that his guilt could not stand in the way of working for the good of those who were suffering. As his biographer commented, "To maintain one's innocence in a setting such as that of the Third Reich, even to the point of not plotting Hitler's death, would be irresponsible action," for, "To refuse to stand with others trying desperately to topple the perpetrators of mass crimes . . . would be the selfish act of one who cared for his own innocence, who cared for his own guiltlessness, more than he cared for his guilty brothers."[53] Bonhoeffer knew that to be part of a communal body, he had to do whatever he could to end the ongoing pain and suffering in that body. For Bonhoeffer, hungering and thirsting after righteousness meant his own purity and even safety became secondary to the welfare of the community.

This kind of love for others is also modeled by Peeta in The Hunger Games books, especially in Katniss's first real encounter with him. In the months after her father's death, Katniss and her family hover on the brink of starvation, driving her to desperately try to acquire food in whatever way she can. One cold wet day as she is rummaging in trash bins behind homes for scraps, the baker's wife emerges to harshly scold her for doing so. Katniss, weak from hunger, simply collapses in the alley at that point, hopeless. Shortly thereafter she hears the baker's wife yelling again, this time at her son, Peeta, for burning some loaves of bread, making them unsellable. She tells him to feed the charred bread to the pigs, and he walks outside with the mark of her beating across his face. Peeta starts to feed the pigs, but then throws the bread to Katniss instead. For the first time in weeks she and her family have a decent meal that not only fills her belly but helps kindle the spark of hope in her. The next day, as she wonders how she could ever thank Peeta, she notices the first dandelion of the season, reminding her of what her father had taught her about foraging in the forest and enabling her to feed her family. The hope Peeta gives her leads her to the salvation of her family. As Katniss comments, from then on she could never shake the connection between "Peeta Mellark, and the bread that gave me hope, and the dandelion that reminded me that I was not doomed."[54]

Peeta loves Katniss and has ever since he was a young boy. He cannot bear to see the girl he barely knows, but still cares for, suffering from hunger. Knowing that his mother would punish him for deliberately burning the bread, he accepts that consequence as a necessary part of the higher good of loving his neighbor. He does the same after Katniss's escape from the Quarter Quell games while he is in Capitol custody. In a televised interview, the broken and abused Peeta gathers the strength to go off-script and warn the rebels living in District 13 that they will be dead by morning. Even though President Snow quickly orders them to cut filming, it is not before images of the blows Peeta receives are broadcast to the watching world. Broken, disoriented, and yet fully aware that his actions could cost him his life, Peeta places the good of others before his own, giving the residents of District 13 precious extra minutes to get to safety before an air raid begins.

Righteousness is the opposite of selfishness—even well-meaning pietistic selfishness. Living in the ways of the Kingdom is hard and sometimes presents us with painful choices. But living rightly in relation to God's desires has to be about aligning ourselves with God's ways and not simply thinking about ourselves. Much of the time, living in these ways can be as simple as letting go of habits of greed and self-serving convenience for the sake of others. But as the examples of Bonhoeffer and Peeta demonstrate, living in such ways might also call us to sacrifice our very assumptions about right living, or even our own lives. The cost of discipleship, as Bonhoeffer wrote, is high, but becoming the people God created us to be is worth the cost.

It Costs Everything You Are

In truth, there is a cost to all our actions. Sacrificing ourselves for the common good might present one with an obvious cost, but any path we choose as we navigate through life will carry some kind of cost. The Games change people, as does war. People are never the same after engaging in acts of violence against others, but that is something we don't usually want to talk about. In a culture that encourages us to look after our own interests instead of the interests of others, our "right" to choose whatever actions we desire is treated as sacred. Mentioning that any of our personal choices come at a cost undermines the sacredness of choice. Preserving the centrality of personal choice requires our culture to make discussions about the hidden costs of our actions taboo. We want cheap food and clothes without having to know the cost to animals, the environment, and workers involved in their production. In this country, giant agribusinesses have even made it illegal to publish pictures of factory farms that would reveal the true source, and hidden costs, of the food we eat. Similarly, the idea that one might need counseling after an abortion is labeled as offensive since that would challenge the cultural notion that such a choice is consequence-free. Likewise, our culture would rather see soldiers simply as heroes without having to really consider the consequences their actions have for the well-being of the soldiers themselves, for their families, and for the countries to which we've sent them. But just because we try to hide from these costs by labeling them offensive or un-American doesn't make them disappear. People still suffer whether we want to admit it or not.

The citizens of Panem's Capitol also tend to look only after their own interests, without considering the cost to others. The Hunger Games exist, in their minds, for the sake of their own entertainment. Even the death of the tributes is, for them, more about their emotional attachment to that tribute than the actual loss of life. The cost of the Games to the districts, and even the emotional and moral cost to their own souls of treating fellow human beings so cavalierly is not openly, if ever, discussed. So when Peeta breaks that taboo in a televised interview and confesses that to participate in the Games, "To murder innocent people? . . . It costs everything you are" a hush falls across those watching because no one has ever talked about the emotional reality of the Games before.[55]

Not attending to those costs—the wounds inflicted upon people and the world around us—can have dire consequences. One sees this in the illnesses that claim former Hunger Games contestants. Haymitch becomes an alcoholic, and the Games cost Annie, a young woman from District 4, her mental health. She saw her partner beheaded in the arena, triggering a mental breakdown. She won her Games simply because she, being from the fishing district, was able to swim better than the other tributes after the Gamemakers flooded the arena. But the trauma she suffered there haunted her, leaving her mentally unstable.

In writing about the costs participating in war, even necessary or just war, has on service members, scholar Rita Nakashima Brock commented, "The hidden wounds of war do not heal when left unattended; instead, they may fester for years in depression, homelessness, addiction, and a half-lived existence finished by suicide, which doesn't end the suffering for those who knew and loved the one who died."[56] As Veteran's

Affairs clinicians reported in 2009, war (especially the recent wars in Iraq and Afghanistan) causes tremendous harm to soldiers' souls.[57] This moral injury has led to unprecedented suicide rates among veterans: of the approximately 30,000 suicides in the United States each year, 20 percent are veterans (an average of eighteen veterans committing suicide a day).[58] Without an accepted space in our culture to openly discuss the horrors of war or the pain that participating in war causes them, the soldiers suffer in silence.

To ignore the full cost of participating in violence, of taking advantage of workers, or of sacrificing the environment for our immediate benefit is to turn away from seeking the shalom of all. It is impossible to be in right relation with other people if we refuse to let the truth about who they are and how they are suffering be told. To leave them alone to bear the emotional and physical costs of actions they engage in, often on our behalf, does not serve the Kingdom of God.

The Capitol doesn't care if participating in the Hunger Games costs the tributes all that they are, but those who hunger and thirst after righteousness should. The righteous don't accept the King's forgiveness of their debt by insisting that others give everything they are to serve them; the righteous forgive their debtors. To be in right relation with others is to help shoulder their burdens in whatever way we can. This might mean not insisting that others pay such high costs for our benefit in the first place. We can pay fair prices for our food and clothing instead of forcing poor workers to make up the cost of cheap items through low wages and abusive work situations.[59] We can challenge the taboo and start thinking through the moral costs of war, or at least be there to listen to the stories and the struggles of those we ask to fight wars for us, and then continue to help them live with the emotional and physical costs of what they did on our behalf. We can let go of our belief that we are entitled to live in whatever way suits us individually, and start living in ways that seek the shalom of all.

But to be in right relation with others, to live sacrificially for them, we must first be in actual relation with them. It is only when we care enough to learn about sufferings and needs of others that we can work for their well-being. All too often we are clueless not only about their needs, but about how our actions are affecting them. We often are like the Israelites whom Ezekiel had to ask, "Is it not enough for you to feed on the good pasture, but you must tread down with your feet the rest of your pasture? When you drink of clear water, must you foul the rest with your feet? And must my sheep eat what you have trodden with your feet, and drink what you have fouled with your feet?" (Ezek. 34:18-19). We have so many blessings that we don't even realize that our enjoyment of them often harms others. Ezekiel condemns the leaders of Israel for letting such things happen. "You eat the fat, you clothe yourselves with the wool, you slaughter the fatlings; but you do not feed the sheep. You have not strengthened the weak, you have not healed the sick, you have not bound up the injured, you have not brought back the strayed, you have not sought the lost" (Ezek. 34:3-4). While the people were busy caring about themselves, they failed to notice those suffering around them. Being aware of others enough to notice their needs is the first step to righteous living.

And it can't be just those we are close to that we take the time to notice and care about either. I was reminded of this one Christmas season as I was listening to a Christian radio station and heard the DJs discussing the importance of buying gifts that were made in the USA. As they put it, buying Christmas gifts that were made in the USA as opposed to some place like China is a great way that we can show love to our neighbors. That dialogue revealed the common assumption that only people who are like us, or are physically near us, are our neighbors who we are to love. I found myself at the time saying (all right, yelling) out loud to the radio in my car, "But people in China are our neighbors too!" Caring for their well-being means not disowning or rejecting them, but ensuring they are treated with respect and dignity. Putting workers in China out of jobs isn't a way to show them love—advocating for them to be treated with respect and paid fairly in their jobs is. Right relationships don't abandon people, they help them.

But just as ignorance and abandonment of the suffering are not part of righteous living, neither are attempts to remain neutral to injustices in the world. As mentioned earlier, sometimes people are afraid that working to end injustice might expose them to the taint of culture or even the hubris of thinking they can save the world singlehandedly, so they end up doing nothing. Others end up so overwhelmed by the problems or confused as to how to actually help that they too are paralyzed into inaction. But hungering and thirsting after righteousness requires action. Remaining neutral in the face of suffering (for whatever reason) fails to pursue right relations. It is only those that hunger enough after righteousness to actively work toward it that Jesus said would be filled. Despite the uncertainty of the outcome or the hard sacrificial work it requires, these people live in ways that are not only aware of the needs of others, but which work to meet those needs. They are the ones seeking the shalom of the community.

Interestingly, when Peeta is taken into the custody of the Capitol after the Quarter Quell, the worst they can do to him is to realize his deepest fears and turn him into a monster. They inject him with tracker jacker venom, a hallucinogen, to "hijack" his true personality and take away his innate desire to care for others. After he is rescued by the rebels, they realize that he is no longer the Peeta they once knew. His love for Katniss and his desire to protect her has been twisted into rage and murderous contempt. His dislike of violence becomes his pleading with the rebels to stop fighting and accept the Capitol's oppression. Instead of working to heal the pain in others, he manipulates them to dwell on their worst faults and despise themselves. As one of his friends tells him, "[T]hey've replaced you with the evil-mutt version of yourself."[60] It is a life-long journey for him to overcome the effects of the venom. After such torture he has to constantly work at seeing good in others and caring for them, but it is work he is committed to, for deep inside he is still the same Peeta who strove to be in right relation with everyone.

Peeta's hijacking makes me wonder what the world would be like if everyone were so committed to seeking the well-being of others that any failure to do so would prompt others to say we had been replaced with the evil-mutt versions of ourselves. Imagine that world where being aware of the needs of others is so second nature it becomes an aberration to not live righteously toward them. That is the world of the Kingdom of God that we are called to live into—a world where we treat others rightly no matter who they are or where they live. Perhaps we are currently so used to the "evil-mutt" world that to live righteously seems strange or even impossible. Our world tries to convince us to care only for ourselves, to satiate our personal hungers and thirsts despite the cost to others. But, as Jesus promised, it is only those who hunger and thirst after righteousness who will be filled.

Chapter Five
The Merciful: Recognizing the Humanity of Others

"Blessed are the merciful, for they will receive mercy."
~ Matthew 5:7

Give Me One Reason I Shouldn't Shoot You

As a child, it always fascinated me to hear my grandfather tell his Navy stories from World War 2—from how he miraculously saved his landing craft from sinking during the D-Day invasion to his involvement in the secret mission to ferry General Patton's army across the Rhine. But the story that haunted me the most was his unexpected encounter with a German civilian. After crossing the Rhine, the U.S. troops were attempting to secure a town on the German-controlled side when a man suddenly stepped out of a doorway and asked my grandfather for a cigarette. My grandfather stood there shocked at this unexpected appearance, his gun pointed at the man, not knowing whether he was a threat. Eventually, my grandfather started yelling and gesturing at the man to run away, which he did. As a child, that image haunted me and has since defined the complexities of war for me. I had a hard time wrapping my mind around the idea of my grandfather standing there with a gun pointed at someone who was theoretically his enemy, but who actually appeared as just a guy asking for a smoke.

I couldn't help but remember my grandfather's tale as I read in *Mockingjay* of Katniss's experience in the war. As part of the rebels' attempt to take District 2 (which was in league with the Capitol), they devise a plan to capture a mountain stronghold that involves trapping the District 2 troops inside the mountain and using bombs to cut off their air supply. Katniss, remembering her own father's death in a mining accident, is disturbed at being part of a plan to essentially cause a massive mine accident. After the plan is implemented, she sees a few survivors struggling to escape the burning and suffocating mountain and she rushes to them, screaming for the rebels to hold their fire. Although in the midst of the war and desiring to conquer her enemies, she intuitively knows that it is wrong to shoot at people as they are desperately trying to escape a burning tunnel. Despite her good intentions, her actions place her in a position of vulnerability and one of the survivors points his gun at her, saying, "Give me one reason I shouldn't shoot you."[61]

By some standards, my grandfather's and Katniss's actions could be labeled as treason or cowardice. As soldiers, their job is to eliminate the enemy and both of them failed to do so once they came face to face with the humanity of those they were fighting. Their own lives were in danger because of their actions, but they could not help but see the person in front of them as a real human being in need of protection rather than merely an abstract enemy.

By the standards of the Kingdom of God this is not treason, but mercy. We live in a society enamored with an idea of retribution, which asserts that people should get what they deserve, especially if they are our enemies. If someone hurts us or someone we love, or even an idea we hold dear, it is assumed that they then owe us something and therefore must pay. While we see this played out on a large scale in movies all the time (think of the typical Mel Gibson film like *Braveheart* or *The Patriot*), retributive attitudes creep into our daily lives in even the most trivial of ways. For instance, we go out to eat and our steak is overcooked or there's a whiny kid at a nearby table, so we take it out on the server by tipping poorly. Or someone cuts us off in traffic and so we tailgate. Or the decorating committee at church doesn't go with our (brilliant) idea so we take our ball and go play elsewhere. Or a store starts saying "Happy Holidays" instead of "Merry Christmas" and we get offended and call for a boycott. The spirit of retribution insists they must pay, sometimes painfully, for what they have done. Mercy is the exact opposite. Mercy acknowledges that by the standards of the world there may not be a good reason not to shoot, but refuses to shoot anyway.

Our English word *mercy* derives from the Latin word *merces* meaning recompense. To show mercy is to erase the debt between two people, to forgive what is owed by acting as if recompense has already been paid. A merciful person therefore does not respond to an injury by insisting that whoever hurt them must pay for what they have done, but instead forgives the injury, essentially canceling any supposed debt that might have arisen. In a world where retribution is the norm, mercy is both rare and deeply unsettling for those who receive it. Nevertheless, Jesus called the merciful blessed.

Prior to Katniss's extension of mercy toward the survivors escaping the mountain are moments when others show mercy to her. These displays of mercy are always unexpected and yet serve to shape Katniss into the sort of person who chooses to show mercy to others. The most poignant of these occurs during her first Hunger Games when she is caught in a deadly fight as she attempts to capture medicine that Peeta needs to stay alive. Another tribute is about to kill Katniss but is instead herself killed by Thresh, the District 11 male tribute. In this fight to the death, Katniss fully expects Thresh to press his advantage and kill her next. Instead he pauses for a moment and asks about Rue, knowing Katniss had teamed up with her. Katniss tells him how Rue died and how she had sung to her and then covered her with flowers. Hearing these acts of kindness from his supposed enemy confuses Thresh's killing intent. After a moment he lowers the rock he was going to use to kill Katniss and says, "Just this one time, I let you go. For the little girl."[62] Katniss's act of kindness toward Thresh's fellow District 11 tribute transforms her, if only for a moment, from enemy to friend, and she gratefully accepts this unexpected display of mercy.

The expectation of the Hunger Games is kill or be killed, yet Thresh doesn't treat Katniss as expected; encountering her humanity moves him to offer mercy instead. Afterward, Katniss comments to Peeta that outside of the Games she thinks she would have been friends with Thresh. She realizes that she doesn't want Thresh to be killed either, but is afraid to say so aloud since it can be considered subversive to question the Games in such a way. The Capitol insists she play the Games by their rules; mercy has no place in their scenario.

In contrast, Jesus repeatedly urges his followers not to give others the punishment supposedly due to them. He tells his followers, "You have heard that it was said, 'An eye for an eye, and a tooth for a tooth.' But now I tell you: do not take revenge on someone who wrongs you" (Mt. 5:38-39 GNT). In a context where many were eager to violently attack anyone aligned with the Roman oppression, these words challenged their inclination to make others pay. But Jesus's words extended beyond even the political realm to cultural situations. So when a woman accused of adultery is brought before Jesus, he does not insist she receive her due punishment of stoning.[63] Instead he invites any of the men standing there ready to kill her who are without sin to cast the first stone. The men are thus brought face to face with the humanity of the woman before them, and as they recognize a bit of themselves in her, they quietly walk away. The woman is astonished to see her accusers leave and at Jesus's assurance that neither will he condemn her.

Jesus also reinforces merciful living as part of God's Kingdom through his parable of the prodigal son.[64] After the son takes and squanders the inheritance he had demanded from his father, he knows that all he deserves now is to be his father's lowly servant and not his son. Yet when the son returns home, his father runs to meet him, puts his own ring on the son's finger, and calls for a lavish celebration. Instead of giving the son what he deserves, the father, in his love, showers blessings upon him. The older brother, caught in a retributive mindset, is indignant at his father's actions. From his point of view, his brother deserves to live in hardship and poverty for insulting his father and wasting his inheritance. When he challenges his father's acts of mercy, the father tells him they must rejoice for his brother, for "he was lost and has been found" (Lk. 15:32). That relationship of father and son matters far more than the expectation that a wayward son should be cast out. In light of that loving relationship, the father mercifully refuses to give the son what he deserves.

Jesus tried to show his followers that the ways of his Kingdom are radically different than the ways of the world. Retribution, revenge, and giving people what we think they deserve are what the world expects. But seeing others only through the lens of how they have hurt you and what they owe you is not part of God's vision for the world. God loved the world so much that he sent his only son as an act of mercy to ensure that we don't have to ultimately suffer the consequences of the choices we have made. Extending mercy is at the core of Jesus's identity and mission, and thus he repeatedly calls his followers to do the same.

How Different Can It Be, Really?

God loves creation so much that God extends us mercy instead of judgment. This boundlessness of the divine love is what makes mercy possible. The scriptures promise that God will never stop seeing us as beloved children deserving of care, compassion, and respect. Isaiah beautifully asks, "Can a woman forget her nursing child, or show no compassion for the child of her womb?" (Is. 49:15). The passage then assures that even more than a mother who has borne and nursed a child, God will never forget her own children. Because of this, God continually extends mercy even as we continue to hurt God in a myriad of ways. God's mercy essentially declares that his love is stronger than our sin, that no amount of offense on our part can overcome God's high regard for us and God's desire to be reconciled to us.

To be merciful as God is merciful, we must choose to see others as fellow children of God, deserving of love, respect, and mercy. When we forget this, it becomes too easy to slip into patterns of retribution and revenge against those who have hurt or offended us. Often we then begin to label them in ways that deny their basic humanity and refuse to acknowledge our shared kinship in God's family. They become the enemy, or *those* illegals, or homosexuals, or conservatives, or liberals, or sexist pigs, or pagans—labels that reduce people to an idea to be opposed instead of a person worthy of respect. We may have legitimate reason to disagree with certain people or to even work to end their oppressive ways, but when we stop seeing them as people it becomes far too easy to lash out in revenge or hatred instead of trying to respect their dignity even in disagreement.

During her time in District 13, Katniss stumbles upon her friend Gale as he is helping to develop weapons for use against the Capitol. Katniss immediately recognizes some of the traps and snares she and Gale used to use while hunting. But now Gale is using the psychology of those snares in weapons of war against the Capitol. These involve booby-trapping areas that hold needed supplies, endangering children so the parents can then be targeted, and luring people into places of supposed safety in order to destroy them. In short, Gale's plans treat people like mere animals to be slaughtered—much as the Capitol treats the tributes they send to die in the Games. To them tributes are not real children with real families, but disposable creatures to be slaughtered for entertainment. Even the rooms where tributes are made ready to enter the arena are called "the stocks," reinforcing the idea that tributes are no different than livestock to be butchered. Having experienced this first hand, Katniss can't help but comment that Gale's plans seem to be crossing some kind of line. Gale responds with hostility, arguing that he is not treating the Capitol any differently than the Capitol treats them. Gale's is the classic "eye for an eye" retributive mentality.

However, Katniss knows that killing people is not the same as killing animals for food. Immediately after she volunteers to be the District 12 tribute, Gale tries to reassure her about the Games telling her it will be just like hunting. When Katniss replies that she has never killed a person before, he responds, "How different can it be, really?"[65] His question disturbs her as she realizes that, "The awful thing is that if I can forget they're people, it will be no different at all."[66]

Later, as he is developing weapons, Gale seems to take his own advice and forgets that they are intended for people and not just animals to feed his family. Katniss, however, has her experience in the Hunger Games to keep her from ever forgetting the harsh reality of killing people. After killing the boy who killed Rue, Katniss is haunted by his image. Gale's question about the difference between killing animals and people returns to her. Katniss realizes that it is "Amazingly similar in execution. A bow pulled, an arrow shot. Entirely different in the aftermath."[67] She tries focusing on what he did to Rue to help her forget his humanity, but she knows that illusion cannot last forever.

Denying others their humanity, in theological language their status as children of God, is what makes it possible to harm them. Social scientist Alfie Kohn writes,

> In order to kill, one must cease to see individual human beings and instead reduce them to abstractions such as "the enemy." One must fail to realize that each person underneath our bombs is the center of his universe just as you are the center of yours: He gets the flu, worries about his aged-mother, likes sweets, falls in love—even though he lives half a world away and speaks a different language. To see things from his point of view is to recognize all the particulars that make him human, and ultimately it is to understand that his life is no less valuable than yours.[68]

We see this reduction to abstraction in movies all the time. It is rare for the "bad guys" to be portrayed as complex characters with families, hobbies, and real emotions because the filmmakers don't want us to sympathize with them. The most famous examples of this are the Star Wars films. In the original episodes the evil Stormtroopers always wore helmets, serving to dehumanize them. In the more recent prequel television series,

Star Wars: The Clone Wars, however, the troopers are the good guys who work with the Jedi, thus they are often depicted with their helmets off and with individual personalities of their own. The bad guys in *The Clone Wars* are instead utterly dehumanized droids, making it easier for viewers to sympathize with the correct characters.

My grandfather's own decision to treat the German man as a real human being (and not just "the enemy") and not shoot was actually a common occurrence among soldiers. Studies conducted after World War 2 revealed that up to 90 percent of soldiers (on all sides), when faced with killing another human being, could not do it. They would fire their weapon, but deliberately miss because they could not bring themselves to take another human life.[69] These soldiers had been trained to shoot a gun, but not to kill. They, like Katniss, discovered that killing another person is not the same as simply shooting a weapon. Realizing this, during the 1950s the U.S. Army's basic training "sought to lay down reflex pathways that bypassed the inhibitions, by training soldiers to snap-shoot at human-shaped targets that only appeared for a few seconds. They also addressed the problem directly, psyching their young soldiers up until they believed that they actually wanted to kill."[70]

Soldiers of more recent wars have shared that they are shocked at times to realize they have killed someone. They can recall being in a potentially hazardous situation and the next thing they remember is seeing a dead body before them. There are bullets missing from their weapon, so they know they must have fired, but they have no recollection of doing so. They are so conditioned to kill on sight that they don't have a chance to see their opponent as a person, even if that person happens to be an innocent civilian or child in the wrong place at the wrong time. If my grandfather had been trained under today's methods, the man who asked him for a cigarette would not have survived that day. Yet, as many soldiers are realizing, and as Katniss did, the illusion that those they killed are inhuman enemies eventually dissolves, leaving them to struggle with both Post Traumatic Stress Disorder and moral injury—the struggles of returning soldiers are not always just medical or emotional, they are also spiritual.

Turning from the dehumanizing effects of war and looking instead to Jesus, we can see a love that cherishes each and every person, even supposed enemies. Jesus challenged assumptions about the worth and dignity (or lack thereof) of even the Romans, the great faceless enemy of the Jewish people, as well as those that collaborated with them. Jesus called Matthew to be one of his disciples and he honored Zacchaeus by visiting his house for a meal. As tax collectors, both men represented the oppressive Roman Empire and were thus despised by their fellow Jews. But Jesus treated them as real people who had the potential for good. Similarly, when the soldiers came to arrest Jesus in the garden of Gethsemane, they weren't just enemies to resist as some of the disciples wanted to do. Instead Jesus treated them with dignity, even healing the man harmed by Peter's reflexive violence.

By calling for his followers to love their enemies, Jesus reveals that dehumanizing labels have no place in the Kingdom of God. I've always loved the rather snarky bumper sticker, "Loving your enemies implies not killing them," because it gets at this revolutionary aspect of the Kingdom. To love someone is, necessarily, to see them as another human being. Loving our enemies dissolves the dehumanizing labels so we can see them as real people in all their beauty and complexity. And while we might still disagree with them and resist their oppressive actions, it becomes much harder to simply hate and harm them.

Why Do You Care So Much?

The Beatitudes declare that the merciful are blessed because they will receive mercy. Seeing others as fellow human beings instead of as enemies or as those deserving of punishment, irrevocably alters our relationship with them. It doesn't mean that they might not still harm us, as Katniss discovered when she extended mercy to those escaping the mountain, but taking steps toward forming even basic relationships often changes not just how we see the other person, but how they see us as well. Those that extend mercy to others are much more likely to see mercy extended to them in return.

We can see this in Katniss's relationship with her prep team—the ostentatious Capitol stylists whose job is to beautify and prepare Katniss for public appearances leading up to the Hunger Games. Like the typical Capitol citizen, trivial in their passions and accustomed to luxury, they generally think only of themselves. For them, styling the tributes to be killed in the arena is simply a lucrative job that can bring them fame. Katniss has every right to despise these people who pluck, tweeze, scrub, and dress her up for slaughter. But instead she can't help but care for them, even pity them.

Gale, always quick to view anyone from the Capitol as his enemy, challenges Katniss one day asking, "Why do you care so much about your prep team?"[71] At first she thinks he is joking and wonders why she shouldn't care for them. Even though they prepare her for the Games, she tells Gale that, "It's more complicated than that. I know them. They're not evil or cruel."[72] By getting to know them for who they are, Katniss finds that she can't help but extend mercy to them. Even if their acts are despicable, she, unlike Gale, doesn't demand retribution but instead lives in the complexity by showing them compassion.

It is Katniss's nature to show that sort of kindness, so it takes her by surprise when she realizes that by forming a relationship with her prep team, they too come to see her differently. When Katniss returns to the Capitol as a tribute for the Quarter Quell Games, she finds her prep team heartbroken and weeping over the fact that she has to return to the arena. She no longer is just a tribute there to entertain them and bring them fame, she is someone they know, someone who was kind to them. She soon discovers that others in the Capitol are similarly disconcerted with the Quarter Quell, which forces past winners back into the arena. It is a revelation to her that any Capitol citizens would care about the tributes and she concludes that it is because the stylists spend so much time with them that they cannot help but grow to care.

Thinking only of what others owe us and refusing to be in relationship with those who may have hurt us limits our ability to experience the blessing of mercy. But mercy defines the ways of the Kingdom of God—a place where every person is valued for who they are (even as they are called to be transformed into merciful people themselves). In this Kingdom we do not assume that others ought to be punished simply because they have offended us in some way. Instead, like Katniss, we extend kindness and mercy even to those who refuse to show the same to us. In this Kingdom, the covenant God made with Abraham that his people will receive blessings in order that they may be a blessing to others is lived out even amidst those we label enemies.

Instead of despising our enemies and demanding that they pay, the way of mercy prompts us to love and respect others. We can see these two ways of responding played out in the scriptures. After the Israelites were released from the Babylonian exile and permitted to return to Jerusalem, many failed to live up to their identity as children of Abraham. Instead of using their blessing to bless others, or remembering Jeremiah's words that they were to seek the peace and prosperity of even their enemies, they themselves began oppressing others. Their leaders Ezra and Nehemiah in particular illustrate the difference between retributive and merciful responses.

After returning from exile, the Israelites had to deal with the fact that the poor farmers had been left in Judah while the rich, the educated, and the elite had been exiled to Babylon. When those exiles returned to Jerusalem there was severe tension between those who had stayed and simply tried to survive the occupation, and the elite who believed that, as the preservers of the tradition, they were owed the right to live well and resume their positions of political and religious authority. For example, when Ezra returned to Jerusalem, he wanted to restore honor to the city by eliminating the elements in society that didn't meet his standards of racial and religious purity. Discovering that some returning exiles before him had intermarried with the poor and non-Jews who had stayed behind, he tore his clothes and wept. He then called an assembly of all the returned exiles, threatening loss of property and exclusion from the community if they failed to show. As they gathered in the pouring rain (a detail included in the biblical narrative that just adds to the misery of the scene) he told them they must repent of marrying foreign women by casting those women and their children away or else face judgment themselves. For the offense of racial impurity Ezra demanded that these helpless women and children make recompense with their very lives (for as widows and orphans they would now have no means of making a living).

But I love that the scriptures do not let that image of casting women and children away be the final word on the subject of how we are to respond to those we perceive as other and offensive. Instead, the fear-based mandates of Ezra are countered by the response of Nehemiah to the very same poor farmers living around Jerusalem. By the time Nehemiah arrived, a generation later, to help govern and rebuild Jerusalem, things had gotten really bad. Times were hard and the people were struggling to survive—in large part because the exiles who had returned under Ezra thought they had the right to oppress and take advantage of those who had stayed. The oppressed peasants came to Nehemiah to tell him about what was happening, saying, "Now our flesh is the same as that of our kindred; our children are the same as their children; and yet we are forcing our sons and daughters to be slaves, and some of our daughters have been ravished; we are powerless, and our fields and vineyards now belong to others" (Neh. 5:5). The Bible says that Nehemiah burned with anger when he heard of the ways these people were being dishonored and treated as less than real people. In response he approached those who were oppressing the poor and said, "The thing that you are doing is not good. Should you not walk in the fear of our God?" (Neh. 5:9).

Nehemiah realized that the identity of the Jewish people had its roots in the Abrahamic covenant, that to be God's chosen people meant they had to be a blessing to others. It meant letting go of selfishness and extending mercy to all those around them. The scriptures testify that the Israelites under Nehemiah were humbled by their lack of mercy and pledged to stop taking advantage of the people who worked the land, promising to return whatever they had unjustly demanded from them. They learned the hard lesson that to follow God meant choosing to make sure everyone is cared for, even those they perceive as "other."

If Nehemiah had been asked, as Katniss was, why he cared so much for the poor and the outsiders in the land, he would have responded that walking in the fear of the Lord demands it. Walking in God's ways means living that life of mercy. Katniss cares for those who prepared her to be slaughtered. Nehemiah cared for those who had offended his culture's sense of purity. Jesus cared for those who represented the Empire oppressing his people.

Mercy requires that we compassionately care for those everyone else is telling us to despise. In a post-9/11 world, that can mean not affirming calls for revenge or dehumanizing attitudes like the one I've often seen on bumper stickers: "All I need to know about Islam I learned on 9/11." It can mean offering a listening ear to a young woman considering abortion instead of automatically condemning her. Or it can mean offering healing services to soldiers trying to make sense of the actions they committed on our behalf, instead of sentencing them to lonely suffering through our misplaced adulation that demands they act like invincible heroes and not wounded warriors.

Mercy doesn't erase the damage done or the need for healing and redemption, but it does acknowledge that all people, even those who have wronged us, are still children of God and worthy of our respect. Mercy creates the conditions in which healing and redemption can occur. And merciful people are blessed because they form the kind of Kingdom relationships where they too can receive mercy, healing, and redemption when they inevitably come to need it themselves.

Chapter Six
The Pure in Heart: Looking Past Artificial Exteriors

"Blessed are the pure in heart, for they will see God."
~ Matthew 5:8

Put on a Good Show?

Growing up, I was taught that the Beatitude "Blessed are the pure in heart, for they will see God" was about my sex life. As long as I kept my virginity intact until marriage, I would be considered "pure" enough to go to heaven where I would see God. Occasionally the interpretation would be amended to say that by accepting Jesus into my heart I would be made pure so that I could see God in heaven after I died. The blessing and experience of God was always for after I died, while purity was a static state of being in the present. One was either pure or not, and the outward sign of my virginity was the sole evidence of that purity. Either way, the verse had little to do with my heart and the things I cared most deeply about; it was all about allowing others to judge by my outward demeanor whether or not I was a "good girl."

It is probably not surprising that I found this particular Beatitude to be a bit trivial, especially since the interpretation I was given never really meshed with my experience of reality. There were people I knew that were loudly and publically labeled "impure" who were doing amazing work for Jesus (a divorced woman, a youth leader who had had an abortion, a man struggling with understanding his orientation . . .). They were the ones I was often given a warning to never fully trust or admire since they were not truly holy. But then there were those I knew who were held up as the paragons of purity and yet were full of bitterness and unforgiving hearts. It made no sense to me. That is, until I realized two important things: that appearances can be deceiving and that this verse isn't talking about sex.

"Pure" in one sense can refer to the physical state of an object; gold and silver are purified to remove anything in them that is not gold or silver; clothing is washed to purify it from dirt. But the term is also used to describe one's commitment to a cause. Soldiers who are committed to defending their nation are said to be pure in their patriotic devotion. Their hearts seek to assure the well-being of their country and nothing can sway them of that purpose. So too are those who are pure in heart in regard to the Kingdom of God. Those that God deems "pure in heart" commit themselves to the ways of the Kingdom—delivering good news to the poor, bringing freedom to the oppressed, and treating all people with the dignity that properly belongs to image-bearers of the divine. They are wholly, purely devoted to seeing God's dreams realized on earth as in heaven, and commit the passions and purposes of their hearts to that end.

Those whose hearts are intent after the ways of the Kingdom are blessed not simply because they will see God in heaven someday, but because they see where God is working in the world already and choose to join God there now. Being pure of heart is so much bigger than sexual purity or even being forgiven. God has not called us to simply accept a static state of being, but to embody the ways of the Kingdom of God in every moment of our lives. To be pure in heart is a dynamic vocation in which we direct all of our passions and desires after the ways of God. It is to love what God loves and care for those God cares for. It is to resist the ways of the world in favor of the ways of God.

But appearances can be deceiving. Some I had been told to admire as pure were actually working at cross-purposes to the ways of the Kingdom of God, while some of those labeled "impure" were using an outward appearance of conformity to the world's expectations to mask an underlying integrity. In both cases, it was the intent of the heart that mattered most.

Throughout The Hunger Games series, Katniss is frequently judged by her outward appearance instead of the intent of her heart. As soon as she arrives in the Capitol before the Games, she is whisked away to meet her prep team to be remade into their ideal of attractiveness. After winning the Games she is given a full body polish so as not to leave even one flaw on her body, making her appear pure on the outside despite the turmoil she feels within. Others continually try to shape her appearance to manipulate how she is perceived by the public. At one point she is forced to practice various interview personas to see which would most appeal to fans of the Games who might then send her gifts to help her survive in the arena (unsurprisingly, none of the false personalities fit her). Even during the rebellion, those in charge attempt to make her over into their idea of how the Mockingjay, as the symbol of the rebellion, ought to appear. Teams of people work at making her over, writing her speeches, choreographing her appearances make Katniss feel like she is simply being prepared yet again to participate in the Games.

Both the rebels using her as their mascot and the Capitol using her to entertain the masses ignore who Katniss truly is. Her desire to help the oppressed people of the districts is less important to the rebels than how they can manipulate her image to help them to win. At one point she is even told to "get to the Capitol and put on a good show."[73] Their fixation on the outward trappings of power and victory eclipse Katniss's personal motives to end the cruelty of the Games and the widespread starvation in the districts. Yet as others vie for the opportunity to reshape her, Katniss struggles with her own identity and how to define what she cares about most. It is a poignant reminder that appearances can deceive, obscuring and confusing the intent of the pure in heart.

All the Colors Seem Artificial

The Hunger Games series repeatedly confronts us with this juxtaposition between façade and reality. Sometimes what looks perfect on the outside hides corruption within, but at other times the things that present questionable exteriors mask hearts of gold. Ultimately it is what lies underneath that counts.

From the moment the stories begin, we receive reminders that image isn't everything. The people of District 12, although poor and struggling, are kind and take joy where they can find it in life. Although it can be easy for the poor to resent the rich, one of the first encounters in The Hunger Games challenges the notion that such external trappings define a person. Katniss and Gale go (illegally) to sell the strawberries they have gathered to the Mayor of District 12, where they encounter his daughter Madge. Madge is well-to-do and her family holds what little power is to be had in the district, but despite trappings of superior position, she displays a kind and compassionate heart. As the series unfolds, we discover that Madge cares for Katniss and doesn't support the oppressive Capitol simply because her family derives their wealth and power from it. Her aunt died in a past Hunger Games, and it is her aunt's old Mockingjay pin (the symbol of the rebellion) that she quietly, yet subversively, gives to Katniss. Gale readily judges Madge based on the externals of her life, but Katniss looks deep enough to discover that appearances do not always define a person.

Perhaps Katniss is remembering that truth as she enters the Capitol for the first time. She sees the rainbow-colored building that glistened high in the air, yet it all seems not entirely real, as "All the colors seem artificial, the pinks too deep, the greens too bright, the yellows painful to the eyes."[74] These beautifully colored buildings are evidence of the wealth of the Capitol, but the beautiful colors mask the selfishness and greed lurking within. The Capitol's outward appearance hides hearts that have no problem oppressing others for the sake of their own comforts or sending children to fight to the death in the Hunger Games for their own entertainment.

Some of Jesus's harshest words in the Gospels were for those who worked to appear perfect on the outside and yet were full of bitterness in their hearts. When addressing the Pharisees, religious sectarians who believed following the rituals prescribed by Jewish law would purify their souls, Jesus spared no words of condemnation. He told them that though they followed the letter of the law by meticulously tithing even their cooking spices, they had missed the point of it all. The purpose for tithing was to extend justice to the needy, to ensure that all members of the community had enough. Tithing was a means to bless others, but the Pharisees treated it as an end in itself. Jesus takes them to task for focusing so much on the outward ritual that they neglect the principles of faith, justice, and mercy the ritual was meant to serve. In one of Jesus's most pointed statements, he warns them, "Woe to you, scribes and Pharisees, hypocrites! For you are like whitewashed tombs, which on the outside look beautiful, but inside they are full of the bones of the dead and of all kinds of filth. So you also on the outside look righteous to others, but inside you are full of hypocrisy and lawlessness" (Mt. 23:27-28).

In the Kingdom of God people are valued too highly to allow self-righteous acts to become an excuse to judge or neglect others. In the New Creation that Jesus brings, we can't be satisfied with only religious rituals or beautiful façades (like whitewashed tombs); hearts must be transformed until they mirror the very dreams of God. The world Jesus proclaimed this path of transformation to was full of diverse ideas about what it meant to be righteous. In response to centuries of domination by outside empires (Babylonians, Persians, Greeks, Romans), Jewish sects arose with differing ideas about how to be faithful to God in light of such oppression. The Pharisees turned to the law, arguing that one becomes holy by following the rules of Torah as closely as possible. Rome could control the government but it couldn't control their ability to follow the strict purity codes. The Essenes, convinced that to even live amidst the Romans was wrong, fled into the desert to await the end of the world. The Sadducees found earthly salvation by cooperating with the Romans while the Zealots, their polar opposite, plotted armed resistance to the Empire's occupation. While each of these groups at their core possessed a valid desire to be faithful despite living under Empire, in practice many of them began confusing their particular way of practicing their faith with faith itself.

Predictably, Jesus caused quite a stir when he came proclaiming the Kingdom of God as a realm where the habits of religion are seen not as ends in themselves, but as means to serve God and others. For instance, he reminded people that the point of the Sabbath was not just obeying a strict list of forbidden activities. Instead, it was intended as a day for people to find rest, rejuvenation, and reconnection with God, with others, and with their own inner selves. But when Jesus healed a man on the Sabbath, providing him true rest for the first time in years, he was attacked for breaking the commandment.

Jesus confounded the sects of his day in other ways too. He both consorted with and critiqued the Romans, causing those who staked their religious identity on either separation or collusion to be offended by his actions. Even more significantly, Jesus did not defend the honor of his people and fulfill their expectations by stirring up an armed rebellion against the Romans. Instead, Jesus encouraged people to have pure hearts, to care about the ways of God above national pride and autonomy.

Jesus explained to his critics that he had not come to abolish the law, but to fulfill it (Mt. 5:17). His purpose was not to get rid of religion, or tell those different sects their practices were all wrong. But Jesus was quite adamant that what truly mattered were the ways of the Kingdom that demonstrate love to both God and others. Religious practices should serve only to make that Kingdom a reality on earth as it is in heaven. Legalistic adherence to practices that prevent one from extending mercy or seeking justice for the oppressed have no place in the Kingdom. Such a façade needs to be torn down so that a pure heart can emerge. No matter how attractive one's religious exterior may be, if it hides a heart that does not bless others by seeking justice and loving mercy, then it is simply artifice and not a testimony to the Kingdom of God.

Sadly, like the glistening buildings Katniss encounters in the Capitol that were masking oppression, and like those in the religious sects of Jesus's day that missed the mark of genuine purity, the church today often hides an impure heart behind the façade of proper or passionate worship. All too often we get so caught up in how best to live amidst our culture that we end up mistaking our forms of church for the function of the Church. Instead of devoting ourselves to the ways of the Kingdom of God, we let the rituals of church define our identity. While religious rituals can certainly help us witness to God's Kingdom, and are useful tools for shaping us into Kingdom ways like those Jesus addressed, we often mistake those practices for the witness itself, and come to think that the shaping is the end in itself, forgetting to actually live them out in the world. Instead of joining where God is at work in the world, our hearts turn inward to focus only on our own personal practice of the faith and pretend (to ourselves and the world) that this is all that is really necessary.

For instance, it is not uncommon for churches to exert more energy defending their particular style of Sunday-morning worship rituals than they do actually worshipping God by serving others in the world. I've seen manifestos and rants regarding whether liturgical or congregational styles are not just preferred but are actually more proper or pleasing to God. Even within preference groups, I've witnessed arguments over trappings as trivial as vestments, communion ware, and musical instruments. Like the Pharisees tithing their cooking spices while forgetting the purpose of doing so, we in the church often lose sight of what it means to ascribe worth to God (what we are supposed to be doing in worship, or "worth-ship"). We convince ourselves that worship is just about the rituals we perform in church while forgetting to turn our hearts to the ways of God—demonstrating that we find God's ways *worthy* enough to follow. Our façade of worship can be like the whitewashed tombs or glistening Capitol buildings, showing the world a seemingly devout exterior while hiding hearts that are missing the point.

Sometimes the religious façade even works against the Kingdom of God. During the 2012 U.S. Presidential primary, one of the candidates suggested that the United States not treat other countries the way we would not want them to treat us. In other words, he suggested following the Golden Rule that Jesus put forth as a central Kingdom principle. But despite the fact that the audience was mostly self-identified Christians, most booed this candidate's suggestion. Even though they claimed to be followers of Christ, their hearts cared more for the power and might of the American empire than about living in the ways of God.

Jesus's harsh words for those who hid impure hearts behind a veneer of religion echoed the Old Testament prophets who repeatedly called God's people to the sort of worship God truly desires. In Isaiah, for instance, we are told that rituals are meaningless if one's heart is not in the right place. I appreciate how *The Message* puts God's words in Isaiah 1:14-17 into contemporary terms:

> *Quit your worship charades. I can't stand your trivial religious games: Monthly conferences, weekly Sabbaths, special meetings—meetings, meetings, meetings—I can't stand one more! Meetings for this, meetings for that. I hate them! You've worn me out! I'm sick of your religion, religion, religion, while you go right on sinning. When you put on your next prayer-performance, I'll be looking the other way. No matter how long or loud or often you pray, I'll not be listening. And do you know why? Because you've been tearing people to pieces, and your hands are bloody. Go home and wash up. Clean up your act. Sweep your lives clean of your evildoings so I don't have to look at them any longer. Say no to wrong. Learn to do good. Work for justice. Help the down-and-out. Stand up for the homeless. Go to bat for the defenseless.*

Worship should never be a charade. Religion should never be a façade hiding impure (or even misdirected) hearts. For the pure in heart, those who are active in working for God's Kingdom in the world, religion and ritual become supports and tools in that work. Like Madge, who displayed many of the same trappings as found in the Capitol but was pure of heart inside, our forms of religion can be visible representations of people who are passionate about serving God and serving others. But, as Jesus cautioned, woe to any of us who confuse our personal preferences with the manifest Kingdom of God.

So You Do It

While the conspicuous luxury of the Capitol masks underlying oppression, The Hunger Games books also show that less than appealing outward appearances can often hide a pure heart within. Throughout the story, Katniss repeatedly discovers that people whom she is at first inclined to judge are often constructing that outward persona to protect those they love. For most of her life, Katniss only knows Haymitch as the town drunk. She assumes that his victory in the Hunger Games must have turned him into a greedy person who only cares about himself and his alcohol. Katniss sees him differently after she realizes that his stand-offishness stems from his desire not to see others get hurt. He, like Katniss, won his Games in an unconventional way that the Capitol disapproved of. Within two weeks of his win, the Capitol had killed his mother, brother, and girlfriend as punishment. Haymitch realized that if he ever cared for anyone again, the Capitol would likely hurt them too, so he kept to himself, turning to (and then succumbing to) alcohol to cover his sorrow and loneliness. Though a disagreeable and selfish person on the surface, Katniss realizes that at his core all Haymitch wants is to protect others from being hurt.

Similarly, when Katniss first meets Finnick, the exceedingly handsome champion from District 4, she finds him less than appealing. Since his victory, he has had strings of lovers every time he has visited the Capitol. As Katniss critically observes, "Old or young, lovely or plain, rich or very rich, he'll keep them company and take their extravagant gifts, but he never stays, and once he's gone he never comes back."[75] Thus, despite his good looks, Katniss cannot find him attractive. The way he seems to use women reminds her too much of the Peacekeeper forces back in District 12 who take advantage of the extreme poverty by giving food to desperate women in return for sexual favors.

Later, however, she learns that those liaisons were not of Finnick's choosing. He reveals that President Snow would sell his body for exorbitant amounts as a reward to Capitol citizens. As Finnick explains, "If you refuse, he kills someone you love. So you do it."[76] In truth, Finnick loves Annie, another District 4 Games winner rendered emotionally unstable because of her experience in the Games. Because Annie is so defenseless, Finnick knew that to protect her he would have to sacrifice himself to President Snow's plans. Once she learns the truth, Katniss wants to beg Finnick's forgiveness for the way she misjudged him. The playboy persona is not his true self, but merely the person the Capitol forces him to be to protect his loved ones. At his core, Finnick is a caring and committed person who works behind the scenes to end the Capitol's oppressive reign.

Katniss feels guilty for judging Finnick because she too knows what it is like to have to convince the world she is something she is not in order to protect those she loves. Katniss's trick with the berries that kept both her and Peeta alive at the end of the Games is seen by President Snow as an act of rebellion. He blames her for the unrest in the districts and demands that she convince the districts that there wasn't any defiance intended in her actions. As with Finnick, Snow tells Katniss that unless she can quell the unrest in the districts, her family and friends will pay the price. Although it pains and disgusts her, Katniss knows that too many people's lives depend on her acting the way the Capitol wants her to act and so she complies.

Their pure hearts and concern for others motivate Katniss, Finnick, and Haymitch to act in ways contrary to their nature. Throughout history oppressed peoples have done the same in order to survive and protect those they love. Women often choose to stay in abusive situations so they can protect their children. Children forced into debt slavery in places like India are told that their parents will be killed or severely beaten if they do not work hard enough to repay their predatory lenders. In both situations it is out of tremendous love and a desire to protect others that they take on the persona of the submissive and accommodating victim. In a similar manner, persons of color in the United States during the period of slavery and after often felt they had no choice but to accept the dominant culture's lie that they must act inferior to people with white skin. To avoid beatings, lynchings, and arbitrary arrests, not just for themselves but for their family and their community, they often took on a subservient and deferential persona. Knowing what was good, true, and right in the world had to be masked behind an outward acceptance of oppression since they or their loved ones would be punished if they dared challenge the unjust actions of the powerful. To judge such compromises fails to see how those actions actually mask a pure heart.

Katniss doesn't find the freedom to be her true self until after she has failed to convince Snow that she is not rebelliously inclined. At first she despairs that her failure to live a convincing lie will mean the end of all hope and that everything she holds dear will be destroyed. That gives way, however, to a sense of relief that she no longer has to pretend. "If desperate times call for desperate measures," she reflects, "then I am free to act as desperately as I wish."[77] As the saying goes, freedom is just another word for nothing left to lose. When her friend Gale is arrested and publically beaten nearly to death, only the former Games winners, Katniss, Peeta, and Haymitch, are able to help him. Everyone else in District 12 leaves Gale to his fate, their fear outweighing their sense of compassion as they know that to help him would mean their own whipping or death. But Katniss realizes that as Games winners already under the Capitol's watchful eyes, they are the only three people in the district who could risk making such a stand. Once they had already reached a point of potentially losing everything, they were finally able to stand up to those with the power to hurt them and those they love.

In our world too, those with little left to lose are often able to be the boldest in working for God's justice in the world. Standing up to oppression is dangerous. There are often dire consequences, ironically including, but certainly not limited to, accusations of "impurity." When oppression is the norm (at times even established as law), those that resist are often accused of being sinfully rebellious for acting contrary to the ways of society.

However, as the Hebrew midwives discovered when they refused to follow the Pharaoh's command to slaughter all male infants, a sin in the eyes of the world can be faithfulness in the eyes of God. We see examples of this in the early church as well. In Roman culture, women and slaves were considered the property of the male in whose house they lived. It was generally assumed that the man could treat his property any way he desired, so tensions with the dominant culture naturally arose when the early church began embracing the message of Jesus and living out the theology that "There is no longer Jew or Greek, there is no longer slave or free, there is no longer male and female; for all of you are one in Christ Jesus" (Gal. 3:28). The dominant culture observed slaves and masters eating together at the Lord's Supper, women preaching and leading churches (some even foregoing head coverings!), and people being treated with dignity instead of as property.

Unsurprisingly then, the early church was accused of all kinds of "impurities"—licentiousness, treason, atheism, and even cannibalism! Paul even had to ask some churches to have caution in how they exercised their freedom in Christ so as to not unnecessarily offend unbelievers and endanger themselves too much. Women were instructed to comply with cultural customs (like covering their head) when they preached and slaves were cautioned to obey their masters. At the same time the fledgling church was encouraged to undermine social injustices by telling both wives and husbands to submit to one another in love (a far cry from husbands treating wives as property) (Eph. 5:21) and telling masters to treat slaves as brothers and equals (Philemon

15-17). Early believers resisted unjust economics by holding their possessions in common (Acts 2:44-45).

Being pure in heart required the early church to resist the ways of the world, a process they had to navigate carefully, lest the culture retaliate too harshly against them. Though wary of compromising their commitment to the way of Jesus, the early church had a lot to lose by challenging the injustices around them. Sometimes their subversive respect for the dignity of all peoples (even women and slaves) had to be hidden behind a façade of superficial adherence to cultural norms, while other times their unconcealed commitment to the Kingdom of God over and against the dominant culture led to their martyrdom. The pure in heart may be blessed, but they rarely have it easy.

This tension between resistance and compliance played out frequently during the Civil Rights movement in the United States. In light of the systemic racism of segregation that treated African Americans as second class citizens, those that sought to uphold the value and dignity of all people often found themselves, like the early church, with no choice but to stand in opposition to the system. To challenge laws saying that people of color must give up their seats to white people and sit in the back of the bus, Rosa Parks refused to move. To demonstrate the injustice of "No Blacks Allowed" signs in stores and restaurants, young black students peacefully occupied those forbidden spaces. These non-violent acts of civil disobedience were a living affirmation of God's Kingdom values, as they called for all God's children to be treated with the dignity and respect that they deserve. As Martin Luther King, Jr. explained to the critics of such tactics, "An individual who breaks a law that conscience tells him is unjust, and who willingly accepts the penalty of imprisonment in order to arouse the conscience of the community over its injustice, is in reality expressing the highest respect for law."[78]

Of course, many of these critics automatically dismissed and condemned the Civil Rights protestors, no matter how just their cause, simply because they refused to obey the law. That many of these critics, like many of the demonstrators, also labeled themselves "Christians" made it all the more difficult for the Kingdom of God to be truly manifest. In their view, like the Pharisees condemning Jesus for healing on the Sabbath or President Snow condemning Katniss for disrupting the stability of Panem, abiding by the law (even unjust laws) was the utmost priority. Anyone who challenged the law or dared to resist it could not possibly be a good person. Strict adherence to the law thus became the excuse that hid an oppressive heart and allowed injustice to flourish. But it was those whose hearts yearned after the ways of God so much that they felt compelled to stand against injustice regardless of what the law said who won the victory against segregation and set the United States on the long road toward racial reconciliation. They knew that having a pure heart, pure enough to drive them to courageous action, was what truly mattered.

Seeing and joining where God is at work in the world can be a messy endeavor. At times, those who have such pure hearts might find that the only way to care for others is to appear to accept the unjust ways of the world. At other times, their commitment to the Kingdom of God will appear subversive and dangerous to the powers that be, and the world will condemn them. But appearances can be deceiving. As God reminded the prophet Samuel, "the Lord does not see as mortals see; they look on the outward appearance, but the Lord looks on the heart" (1 Sam 16:7).

Chapter Seven
The Peacemakers: Subverting the Games of Violence

"Blessed are the peacemakers, for they will be called children of God."
~ Matthew 5:9

Nothing Ever Changes

I recently saw a car displaying a bumper sticker that read "To Hell with our Enemies! God Bless America." At the time I found it fairly disturbing that anyone would want to display such a hateful sentiment on their car. It also made no sense to combine those two sentiments, since they directly contradicted the message of Jesus who instructed us to "love your enemies, do good to those who hate you, bless those who curse you, pray for those who mistreat you" (Lk. 6:27-28). Seeking the destruction of others and hoarding God's blessing for ourselves, while a common attitude in our culture today, has no place in the lives of those who choose to follow in the ways of God's Kingdom.

Perhaps that is why Jesus announced that it is the peacemakers who will be called "children of God." Those that actively work to do good to others, even those that hate them, are obviously living in the way of the Kingdom. To the outside observer, peacemakers are the most visible children of God. But sadly, being a peacemaker is something that few in our modern world would call "blessed." Too often peacemakers are confused with pacifists, and while there may be times and places for pacifism, peacemaking is different because it requires an active rather than passive relationship with the world.

Peacemakers do not withdraw from relationships with violent people or shy away from conflicts, but instead engage in the work of healing and restoring broken relationships. They live a life that seeks to undo injustices, forsake revenge, and actively care for others. Those who choose this life can see the ways they have done violence to others and seek to make amends for their behavior. They seek to find more creative and loving ways to deal with situations where violence is usually the default approach. Choosing to be a peacemaker means not just abandoning the way of violence, but deliberately living a life that seeks justice and reconciliation.

Peacemakers are children of God because they embody the opposite of violence. By definition, violence involves actions or words that damage or abuse others. At the core of the word is the word *violate*. To violate something is to desecrate or profane it; in other words, to disrespect the very nature of what that thing was intended to be. Violence toward others sends the message that the other person does not deserve respect, is not worthy of our compassion and love, and should not be treated as an image bearer of God. Peacemaking, as the very embodiment of the ways of God, can't help but work to counter these dehumanizing effects of violence. But as Katniss discovered, even with good intentions at heart it is hard to avoid getting caught up in cycles of violence.

When confronted with the cruelty and oppression of the Capitol, Katniss is rightfully angry. Forced to suppress her anger most of her life for fear of being punished, it is Rue's death that finally pushes her to do something about her anger at the injustices the Capitol inflicts upon the people of Panem. Her first impulse is to take revenge on the Capitol, and when she is claimed by the leaders of the rebellion in District 13 Katniss quickly joins their cause. She trains as a soldier and is equipped with special weapons capable of taking down Capitol hovercrafts. But the allure of revenge soon fades as she begins to wonder what sort of world it is that she is fighting for. Her comment to Rue that "Destroying things is much easier than making them" holds true even for the rebellion.[79] As she is swept along the path of violence, Katniss cannot help but question whether she is truly building a better world.

During one of the televised interviews the Capitol has with the captured and tortured Peeta he begs Katniss to use her influence to stop the war before it is too late, asking her if she really even trusts the people she is working with. While the people around her dismiss Peeta's words or condemn him as a traitor, his question forces Katniss to deal with the unease she feels amidst the District 13 rebels. She observes that the leaders of District 13 can be just as cruel and controlling as those in the Capitol and that in some ways District 13 may even be more controlling than the Capitol as dissent of any sort is not tolerated. The President of District 13, Alma Coin, is aptly named as she represents simply the other side of totalitarian oppression. Like President Snow in the Capitol, she too hungers after power, and her actions reveal she can be just as cruel and ruthless as him. She has Katniss's stylists locked away in inhumane conditions simply for being Capitol citizens and later, after taking the Capitol, she proposes sending the children of Capitol officials to die in a Hunger Games to satisfy the need for vengeance with the least loss of life. At Coin's proposal Katniss can't help but think, "All those people I loved, dead, and we are discussing the next Hunger Games in an attempt to avoid wasting life. Nothing has changed. Nothing ever changes."[80]

Katniss's despair at Coin's display of cruelty mirrors the hopelessness she expressed when the District 2 soldier escaping the imploding mountain held her at gunpoint and asked for a reason not to shoot her. With his gun pointed at her, she replies, "I can't. That's the problem isn't it . . . We blew up your mine. You burned my district to the ground. We've got every reason to kill each other. So do it. Make the Capitol happy . . . It just goes around and around, and who wins? Not us. Not the districts. Always the Capitol. But I'm tired of being a piece in their games."[81] Violence begets violence. As Katniss loses nearly everything she loves to the violence, she comes to realize the futility of games of revenge. For that is all it is—a game.

When she and Finnick, having survived being used as pawns in two Hunger Games, see the hologram of the battlefield they will face in their attempt to invade the Capitol, they realize that the war is just like the Games. As in the arena, the streets of the Capitol are laced with deadly obstacles designed to either kill or trap the rebel invaders. The war is just another round in the same dehumanizing cycle of violence, and Finnick and Katniss realize they are once more being sent as pawns to fight in the Games. For, just as in the Games, all that matters to those in power is that they cling to their positions of power, not how many lives are lost.

The cycles of violence that Katniss gets trapped within are familiar stories in our world. All we have to do is watch the nightly news or look to our popular movies to see that revenge and retaliation drive the narratives. We can even see the devastating effects of cycles of violence in the Bible. Take the story of Samson for example. Set within the context of the Philistine rule over Israel, Samson repeatedly resorts to violence and revenge. At his wedding to a Philistine woman he gets tricked, retaliates by killing thirty men, and "burning with anger" apparently abandons his wife. When she is given to another man he proclaims, "This time I have a right to get even with the Philistines; I will really harm them" (Judg. 15:3 TNIV). Samson destroys the crops, olive trees, and vineyards (the entire economic base) of the Philistines, who retaliate by burning Samson's wife and her father to death. To that offense Samson vows, "I won't stop until I get my revenge on you" (Judg. 15:7) and we are told that he then viciously slaughters many of them. His prowess and destruction of the Philistines earned him the approval of the Israelites, who set him up as their leader. Although we often tell his story to children, coating it with moralistic overtones and usually presenting Samson as a hero, we forget that the Bible summarizes these stories of the judges with "In those days Israel had no king; everyone did as they saw fit" (Judg. 21:25). There was no higher guidance to keep the people on the path of righteousness, so instead they played their games of revenge and violence with only concern for themselves.

Jesus delivered his message into a culture similarly plagued with vengeful violence. In the 2nd century B.C.E., the Maccabean rebels engaged in a prolonged and bloody guerilla war in an attempt to purge Israel of Greek domination. The Maccabees laid siege to the citadel of Jerusalem, starving the people inside until they relinquished the city. Those considered tainted by Greek culture were expelled from the city, and the warriors, who saw themselves as pure Jews, entered the city "with praise and palm branches, and with harps and cymbals and stringed instruments, and with hymns and songs, because a great enemy had been crushed and removed from Israel" (1 Macc. 13:51). Some hailed Judas Maccabee as the Messiah—a Hebrew word designating an anointed king of Israel. When the Maccabees' dynasty fell to Rome in 63 B.C.E., many Jews looked for another Messiah who would lead a similar revolution against the Romans. Instead Jesus came anointed by God to teach love for one's enemies and that peacemakers are blessed, calling his people back to the Abrahamic covenant of their being a blessing to the nations. Just like the Maccabees, he rode into Jerusalem amidst praise and palm branches, but on a donkey, not a war horse. Then, instead of expelling the Gentiles and Greek-influenced Jews, Jesus went to the Temple and quoted from Isaiah: "for my house shall be called a house of prayer for all peoples" (Is. 56:7). The contrasts could not be more apparent.

Jesus didn't simply acquiesce to the Romans (more on this next), but he also doesn't seek violent and dehumanizing revenge. As biblical scholar Wes Howard-Brook writes, "The way of empire has always been to justify the escalation of the cycle of violence, as seen so tragically in the aftermath of 9/11. The Romans made an art of the kind of 'scorched earth' policy that 'taught a lesson' to people who would dare resist imperial authority. Jesus reverses this completely".[82] In the face of the Romans' violent oppression Jesus doesn't call for more violence. When Peter responded with violence in the Garden of Gethsemane, Jesus chose to make amends and serve by healing. He told Peter, "Put your sword back into its place; for all who take the sword will perish by the sword" (Mt. 26:52).

It took heartbreak and pain for Katniss to realize that escalating cycles of violence are a game the powerful play that only ends up hurting the most vulnerable. Jesus modeled an alternative way of peacemaking that worked for transformation without relying on vengeance or violence. And he called the children of God to be peacemakers along with him.

It Benefits No One to Live in a World Where These Things Happen

As Jesus demonstrated, working for an end to oppression does not mean adopting the same violent strategies as one's oppressors. Katniss lost hope in the rebellion when she realized that the District 13 rebels were no different that the Capitol leaders. Sadly, this is often the result of violent rebellions throughout history. Regimes are overthrown, but the formerly oppressed often end up looking like their oppressors as they adopt the same tactics to sustain their newly acquired power. There is something about using violence as a means of change that tends to corrupt the ends. As Walter Wink commented, "This pattern of centralized power-holding is not easily renounced after victory is won. After assuming power, ideological differences within the movement are dealt with by the same methods used to gain power; exterminations, purges, torture, and mass arrests."[83] For instance, when Katniss's questioning of the rebel's tactics begins to get in the way of President Coin's plans, Coin arranges for Katniss to be sent into a battle situation that will likely result in her death. As she struggles to overthrow a totalitarian government, another is right there waiting to take its place.

Once Katniss realizes that the rebellion will change nothing, she does the only thing she can think to do—continue the violence by killing President Coin. She fully expects to be executed for her act, but it is the only way she can think of to avoid another oppressive government. Overwhelmed by the futility of violence, she just wants to escape the never-ending cycle of revenge. She declares that she will never again be the pawn of the powerful or use the weapons they design for her to use on their behalf. She despises being a human being "because something is significantly wrong with a creature that sacrifices its children's lives to settle its differences. You can spin it any way you like . . . But in the end, who does it benefit? No one. The truth is, it benefits no one to live in a world where these things happen.[84]

After all she had experienced, Katniss assumes more violence and death are the only way to be free of the system that disgusts her. Acting on that assumption drives her to near insanity and a deep depression that nearly ends her life. But the truth is that the cycle of violence is not inescapable, for, as Jesus demonstrated, resisting oppression does not have to be violent. Peacemakers actively work for a better world, yet seek to do so in ways that do not violate the dignity of those involved.

Under the harsh occupation of the Romans, the Jews had little control over their own lives. A Roman soldier, the embodiment of the controlling power of the government, could demand that any Jewish person carry his pack for one mile. A mile was the farthest they could demand a person to go, but the packs were extremely heavy and the effort forced people to neglect their own work, something the poor could ill-afford. Jesus knew that to refuse to carry a soldier's pack would result in punishment, if not death. So instead he encouraged the occupied Jews to literally go the extra mile, carrying the soldier's pack beyond the legal limit. A soldier could face discipline for conscripting a civilian for more than a mile, so by going further with the pack the soldier would have to beg for it back, putting him in a position of needing something from a Jew. Such a reversal of roles undermined the assumed superiority the Empire held over its conquered peoples, forcing the soldier, at least for a moment, to treat the Jewish person not just as an inferior to be used, but as equal to be engaged with. It was a way to respond without violence, but also without simply accepting oppression.[85]

Creatively exposing oppressive acts for the shameful things they are preserves the dignity of the oppressed while simultaneously calling the oppressor to a more dignified way of being. For oppressors to repent of their actions, they first must become uncomfortable with them, realize how undignified they have become. As Walter Wink writes, "The Powers That Be literally stand on their dignity. Nothing depotentiates them faster than deft lampooning. By refusing to be awed by their power, the powerless are emboldened to seize the initiative, even where structural change is not possible."[86] Acts of creative non-violent subversion provide what Wink refers to as a "third way" between fight or flight. He admits that sometimes such a third way may not be possible and violence perhaps necessary, but that always seeking out such a third way first can help put an end to cycles of unnecessary violence that destroy the dignity of all involved. Such third ways are how we as peacemakers can love our enemies and still work for the transformation of the world.

The Boldest Form of Dissent

Although Panem eventually descends into violent rebellion, the most powerful acts of resistance in the books are those that embody this third way of creative subversion. After Katniss volunteers as tribute in place of her sister, Effie, the woman running the District 12 Reaping, horrifically calls for a round of applause. But not a single person claps. As Katniss observes, "I stand there unmoving while they take part in the boldest form of dissent they can manage. Silence. Which says we do not agree. We do not condone. All this is wrong."[87] They could not protest, but neither would they agree to celebrate the sending of Katniss to what seemed like near certain death. They chose a third way.

Similarly, when past winners are being presented as tributes once again before the Quarter Quell, they do not quietly submit. Although they know they have no choice but to fight again, this time they know what to expect and will not play the part the Capitol expects of them. In most Games the tributes accept that they are each other's enemies to kill or be killed as the Capitol demands, so they treat each other as enemies from the moment they gather. It is a way of keeping the districts divided and the Capitol in complete control. But in their final appearance before the Quarter Quell, the past victors join hands and, as Katniss describes, "[A]ll twenty-four of us stand in one unbroken line in what may be the first public show of unity among the districts since the Dark Days."[88] The Capitol immediately stops the broadcast, turning all the screens dark, but not until that image of solidarity has been seen by all.

Most poignant is the creative undertaking of Katniss's stylist Cinna. Although a brilliant stylist and clothing designer, Cinna is not caught up with the same trivialities as others in the Capitol. He does not dress flamboyantly, dye his skin unnatural colors, or alter his body with whiskers in the manner of other trend-obsessed Capitol citizens. Neither does he seek fame like the other Games stylists, instead seeking an assignment to the lowly District 12. He exists in the world of the Capitol, but is not consumed by its ways or distracted by its circuses. Instead he works from within as an agent of change. When President Snow demands that in her final interview Katniss wear the wedding dress she would have worn in her wedding to Peeta, Cinna gives into the request, but not without making a few changes. Snow's demand is an attempt to assert his control over every aspect of the tributes' lives, so Cinna reminds Snow that there are some things he cannot control. Cinna alters Katniss's dress so that when she raises her arms and twirls for the crowd, it burns away to reveal a Mockingjay dress beneath. In front of all of Panem Katniss stands there as the symbol of everything the Capitol cannot control, the symbol that has come to represent the resistance. This act of creative subversion costs Cinna his life, but brings the districts of Panem together in a way that ends up changing everything.

As with Jesus's suggestion about walking the extra mile, these creative solutions are acts of peacemaking that seek to balance inequalities the world has imposed upon God's beloved children. The powerful are brought down from their assumed positions of superiority and the oppressed are uplifted, creating a space where each can see the other as dignified children of God. As Mary sings in her hymn of praise after learning she would be the bearer of the Messiah, her soul magnifies the Lord because he has brought down the mighty from their thrones and exalted those of humble estate. She recognizes that in the Kingdom of God there exist no such hierarchies of worth, a reality that is made manifest in Jesus and yet is also the ongoing task of the people of God as we strive to see it realized in our world today. Peacemakers are those who live into that task by finding the creative solutions that manifest the Kingdom of God without betraying its values.

For instance, in addressing how a peacemaker might respond creatively to the threat of terrorists in our world, Christian activist Jim Wallis compares it to draining a swamp.[89] If there is an epidemic of malaria one could provide medicine and mosquito nets to prevent the spread of the disease, or one could eliminate the conditions that cause an epidemic by draining the swamp where the mosquitoes breed. He suggests that a more effective solution than hunting down terrorists with armies (which tends to only create more terrorists) would be to instead address the conditions that breed terrorism in the first place—things like poverty, hunger, and the lack of education and opportunities are what make people desperate enough to think violence is their only way to reclaim their dignity.

Or take the example of the women who saved the country of Liberia.[90] That country's dictator, Charles Taylor, in his greed for money and power, ruled by means of his roaming military bands, which had no regard for human rights (funding their operations by trafficking blood diamonds and sex slaves). The opposing warlords cared little for saving the country, and made use of the same injustices to secure power and wealth for themselves. The women were tired of seeing their husbands and sons sacrificed to the ongoing violence, of watching their children starve, of having to flee their homes, and of witnessing the rape and murder of family members.

But instead of simply despairing or joining on the violence, they took a stand for peace. Taking their cue from the biblical story of Esther, they wore simple clothes and began protests for peace, hoping to gain the attention of President Taylor and the warlords. They occupied the fish markets, holding signs, singing songs, and even persuading their priests and imams to join their cause. They even withheld sex from their husbands until they would listen to reason. The warring factions eventually agreed to meet for peace talks, which involved all the men secluding themselves in the Presidential Palace at the expense of international peacekeepers. It soon became apparent that the men were not even pretending to negotiate, but simply taking advantage of the nice accommodations, so the women staged a sit-in at the palace, blockading the men in with their bodies until a decision was reached. Even when the chance of democratic elections was won, they campaigned still—guiding the disarmament process, getting women out to vote, and electing for Liberia the first female president of any African nation. Committed to making peace, these women used all of their strength and creativity to save those they loved from their own enslavement to cycles of violence.[91]

Sometimes oppression doesn't come in the form of outright violence, but is found in systems that nevertheless cause harm to others. For example, in December of 2010 a number of churches in the city of Cudahy, Wisconsin were trying to get permission to offer shelter to the homeless during severely cold weather. The city, citing zoning codes, refused to let the churches become shelters for the homeless, even as unseasonably cold weather dropped temperatures into the deadly single digits. At this point two area churches decided that keeping people alive was far more important than getting bogged down in the red tape of zoning laws, so they started offering "all-night prayer services" to the homeless in their town. The services offered a hot meal as well as bathrooms and showers. And, as the pastor of one of the churches mentioned, if people "happened" to fall asleep at the prayer service, "It wouldn't be the first time people fell asleep in church."[92] The churches knew their creative solution subverted the laws of the city, but they also knew that keeping people alive was far more important than abiding by a code that told them they couldn't help people.

Such real life stories of creative third way solutions inspire hope that the cycles of violence (physical or bureaucratic) are not inevitable. At times, however, the creative solutions that bring down the powerful and uplift the oppressed can only be found in fictional depictions of the way we wish reality had unfolded. Such depictions can be seen as hopeful imaginings— telling the truth about how the world should work by creatively juxtaposing it against the starker reality of how it usually does.

Take, for instance, the elaborate hoax arranged by the Yes Men group in 2004 to mark the 20th anniversary of the Bhopal Disaster. The 1984 gas leak at the Union Carbide pesticide plant in Bhopal, India is considered one of the worst industrial disasters in history.[93] The leak caused thousands of deaths within the first week and is cumulatively responsible for over 25,000 deaths and 500,000 injuries and disabilities. Minimal aid was given to those affected by the plant and the U.S. Supreme Court declared that Indians could not hold the U.S. owners of the plant responsible for negligence and poor working conditions. Because of this, the people of Bhopal suffered for years from severe medical conditions, a toxic environment, and little hope. Thus, when in 2004 a "Jude Finisterra"[94] appeared on the BBC as a representative of Dow Chemical (who now owns the plant) to declare that they were finally accepting full responsibility for the incident and providing a settlement to provide medical care and environmental clean-up, the people of Bhopal rejoiced.[95] They had been waiting twenty years for justice, and this news was their first sign of hope in a very long time.

It was quickly revealed, however, that the statement was a hoax and that Dow had no intention of claiming responsibility or helping the people of Bhopal. The BBC issued an apology to Dow and the Yes Men were chastised for bringing false hope to the people of Bhopal. Nevertheless, the people of Bhopal later said they appreciated the stunt for bringing attention to their plight, an injustice most of the world has sadly forgotten. At the same time, Dow Chemical was publically forced to face the shame of their real-world irresponsibility and compassionless inaction. The Yes Men let the watching world briefly glimpse the way things should have been—with the suffering and oppressed being cared for instead of being forced to bear the brunt of a disaster inflicted upon them by those the world refuses to hold accountable.

Another great example of this use of fiction to imagine a better world is the Jim Carrey movie *Fun with Dick and Jane* (2005). After losing his job and retirement funds in the collapse of an Enron-like company, Carrey's character pulls a Yes Men-like stunt by holding a press conference announcing that the company's CEO will personally reimburse the retirement funds of the jobless employees who lost it all. When the CEO is surprised at his house by the press conference and surrounded by cameras and people thanking him, he has to go along with the scheme. Since reality failed to provide justice for actual Enron workers, this film had to present the way things should have been after Enron's collapse.

The same kind of thing also happens in the music video to U2 and Green Day's song *The Saints Are Coming.* In the video one sees images of a Katrina-ravaged New Orleans, but then fake headlines of "US Troops Redeployed from Iraq to New Orleans" flash across the screen. Images of bombers dropping aid packages and rescuing children from the floods along with the mesmerizing refrain of "the saints are coming" are undeniably hope-inspiring. People know this is how it should have been—an all-out, no-holds-barred mission of aid and hope. The video ends with the sign "not as seen on TV," reminding viewers that reality did not live up to what we hoped it would. Nevertheless, the creative impulse of hopeful re-imagining is itself a form of hope that a better world is still possible. Peacemakers are those who cling to that hope and work for that imagined world.

At the bitter end of Katniss's first Hunger Games, when the Gamemakers revoke the rule that there can be two survivors, Katniss and Peeta understand that one of them must die for the other to survive. But instead of being forced into making this horrific choice, Katniss calls the Gamemakers' bluff as both she and Peeta prepare to swallow poisonous nightlock berries in an attempt to commit mutual suicide. The ruse works and they both are rescued at the last minute. But Katniss's creative subversion of the Gamemakers' intended violent end infuriates the powers that be. Haymitch warns Katniss that the Capitol is furious about what she did in the arena because "The one thing they can't stand is being laughed at and they're the joke of Panem."[96] The powerful are brought down, the oppressed uplifted, and violence avoided, at least for the moment, by Katniss's creative third way.

Katniss must try to convince the world that her act was done out of passionate love for Peeta and not outright rebellion. But, in truth, it is love that drives all acts of resistance to oppression. Like the women in Liberia who loved their husbands and sons too much to continue to see them sacrificed to never-ending war, love pushes people past the problematic responses of fight or flight into the creative third way of peacemaking. Those who truly love their neighbor cannot abide their suffering and therefore choose to live in ways that subvert injustice and uplift the oppressed. They don't resign themselves to a "that's just the way the world is" attitude, nor do they violently respond to injustice with more injustice. Instead, respecting the dignity of all peoples, they do the hard work of finding realistic yet creative alternatives. It is easy to see how they practice the ways of the Kingdom of God—how they are living as the children of God. And for that Jesus called these peacemakers blessed.

Chapter Eight
The Persecuted: Finding One's Voice in a Distracted World

"Blessed are those who are persecuted for righteousness' sake, for theirs is the kingdom of heaven."
~ Matthew 5:10

I've Never Been in Such a Dangerous Place in My Life

In my book *Everyday Justice*, I present evidence about how most of the chocolate we consume has connections to human trafficking and child slavery. I encourage readers to think about where they choose to spend their money and to seek out ways to stop financing child slavery through their candy purchases, which might involve buying chocolate from companies that use fair labor practices (even when they cost more). Out of all the suggestions I give for how we can seek justice with our everyday actions, this is the one people seem to have the hardest time accepting.

I frequently receive emails or am approached by people telling me that I have completely ruined chocolate for them. The treat they used to enjoy now fills them with guilt since they know children suffered to provide it for them. Most people tell me this with chagrin, as they have resigned themselves to paying the extra money and putting in the effort to find slave-free chocolate (even if it means they eat it less often). But a few of these people are genuinely angry with me for exposing them to the truth. They are more upset that they can no longer enjoy their indulgences guilt-free than they are that children are often kidnapped and forced to work as slaves in the cocoa fields. Their entitlement to luxury is more important to them than the ability of those children to live as healthy and whole people.

Attitudes like this reinforce for me how alien the Kingdom of God is to the ways of the world. When people are angered by the suggestion that they should give up a minor luxury for the sake of others, it sheds light on why those who live in the ways of the Kingdom are so often persecuted. Loving others, treating all people with the dignity they deserve, and looking out for the needs of all people are not the ways of the world. Those that live in those ways, who claim citizenship solely in God's Kingdom, are by definition outcasts of the world and will often face mockery, anger, sanctions, and reprimand. Jesus calls those who dwell in the Kingdom blessed, but the world often only despises and persecutes them.

It is easy to forget that persecution for righteousness' sake takes many forms. There are many tragic stories of Christians tortured or killed in countries that have laws against Christianity. Simply admitting to following Jesus in those settings is enough to bring persecution upon a person. The extremes of those stories often cause us to forget that following Jesus involves much more than simply admitting to our faith. It also involves challenging our culture in ways that are sure to invite persecution.

Many Christians have become confused about what it means to be persecuted for following Christ. These days many will actually claim to have been persecuted simply because they have to acknowledge or interact with people who believe or live differently than themselves. They call it persecution to be told they have to respect people of other religions or allow people of all sexual orientations to be openly acknowledged in public. But it is not persecution to be told that your coworker or classmate doesn't share your religious or moral convictions and yet you still have to be nice to them. Ironically, what they see as persecution is actually what Jesus called living in the ways of the Kingdom—loving and respecting those that are different because they too are children of God.

As mentioned earlier, the English words "righteousness" and "justice" are both valid translations of the same Greek word (*dikaiosune* in this Beatitude). Our modern distinctions between the two often confuse our understanding of what it means to be persecuted for righteousness sake. Past readers grasped their connectedness more readily. On how the meaning of these terms has altered over time, philosopher Nicholas Wolterstorff notes, "Apparently, the translators were not struck by the oddity of someone being persecuted because he is righteous. My own reading of human affairs is that righteous people are either admired or ignored, not persecuted; people who pursue justice are the ones who get in trouble."[97] These days persecution for the sake of *justice* extends beyond those killed for claiming the name of Jesus. It also includes those who work to right the wrongs in the world. The persecuted in Jesus's day and our own are those that commit to subverting the ways the world takes advantage of, violates, excludes, and oppresses the beloved children of God. Those who realize that the bread and circuses of society serve to distract us from caring for others and working for justice often become the targets of those who profit from injustice.

Katniss's challenge of the Capitol's main instrument of control makes her a target. Victors of the Games are told to expect a life of ease after winning, but Katniss and Peeta quickly realize they must continue to comply with the Capitol's party line or else face the consequences. After winning the Games, it doesn't take long for Katniss to realize how precarious her situation is. She comments that when she left the arena she thought she was safe for the rest of her life, "But . . . I've never been in such a dangerous place in my life."[98] Challenging the injustice of the Games brought her under the Capitol's scrutiny because, in order to remain in control, the Capitol cannot allow anyone to question its ways. Living counter-culturally, even in minor ways, subverts the power of those that control the culture. The Capitol uses threats and fear to keep the people of Panem in line, but Katniss chooses to value love more than fear. From hunting illegally to feed the people of District 12 to her ruse to save Peeta's life, she deliberately chooses an alternative lifestyle that subverts the Capitol's control. That is why they have to persecute her—threatening her, hurting her emotionally and physically, keeping her under surveillance, trying to humiliate her, and even sending her back to the Games for the Quarter Quell. Acting out of love instead of fear guarantees her such hardships.

Jesus not only calls the persecuted blessed, he promises that those who live according to the Kingdom of God will be persecuted because they are living in culturally subversive ways. These days, however, many Christians (in the Western world especially) are so wedded to the exploitative, consumerist, and self-centered ways of culture that they have become convinced that to resist these ways is itself a sinful act. Instead of calling corporations to stop oppressing and exploiting their workers, some Christians see their ability to indulge in the luxuries those businesses provide as proof of God's blessing.

I've heard church people chastise and mock other Christians who call for banks to stop taking advantage of the poor through unfair lending practices. And I am constantly hearing Christians echo the culture as they say it is their God-given right to make money however they want (no matter who it hurts), keep it all for themselves, and make sure it is not "stolen" from them (in the form of taxes) in order to feed the needy, send children to decent schools, or provide health care for those that can't afford it. Ironically, but not surprisingly, it is those who uphold Kingdom values of loving our neighbors and caring for the poor, who are then accused of selling out to the culture and rejecting Christianity. Persecution takes many forms.

I love how comedian and committed Christian Stephen Colbert addressed this issue of Christians mistaking the ways of the world for the ways of God when he said, "If this is going to be a Christian nation that doesn't help the poor, either we have to pretend that Jesus is just as selfish as we are or we've got to acknowledge that he commanded us to love the poor and serve the needy without condition. And then admit that we just don't want to do it."[99] We often don't want to make sacrifices or face the persecutions (or just the uncomfortable awkwardness) of living counter-culturally. But allowing others to twist scripture to convince us to abandon the Kingdom of God and conform to the world instead is not glorifying to God, no matter how easy or convenient it may be. It is dangerous to seek first the Kingdom of God. Persecution is guaranteed. But those that do are blessed for that very reason.

But We Know How to Dance

Like the readers who were angry with me for ruining their enjoyment of chocolate, we often get so caught up in the distractions of life that we can come to see such things as entitlements. Our right to enjoy every little thing life has to offer becomes so important to us that we can't imagine living any differently. The idea of living sacrificially for the sake of others, or even not having access to the things we enjoy, becomes so unacceptable in our eyes that there is no danger of choosing to live in ways that are even marginally counter-cultural. If it means we have to give up (or simply limit) our clothing addiction, or our chocolate indulgence, or our technology in order to stop the suffering of workers or put an end to child slavery, we often are not willing to make the sacrifice. Those that profit from the ill-treatment of others have no need to persecute us for questioning their control; they know that we are so accustomed to our bread and circuses that we don't care enough to bother.

For instance, in early 2012 there were a number of news stories about the harsh and abusive working conditions of the workers in the factories that manufacture Apple products. These conditions had been in the news repeatedly over the past four years, but consumers had done little to pressure Apple to improve conditions. As one Apple executive explained to the *New York Times*, "You can either manufacture in comfortable, worker-friendly factories, or you can reinvent the product every year, and make it better and faster and cheaper, which requires factories that seem harsh by American standards . . . And right now, customers care more about a new iPhone than working conditions in China."[100] Thus, according to this Apple representative, since there is more demand for the latest gadget than there is for justice, the company sees no obligation to treat their workers well. Sadly, that executive is almost certainly right about the apathy of the American consumer.

Those whose wealth and power derive from exploiting the weak know the masses will not protest such actions if it requires them to sacrifice the luxuries they have come to expect. And as the ancient Romans knew, keeping the masses entertained also keeps them subdued. It's a strategy any parent is familiar with. The easiest way to get a whiny, demanding child to be quiet so you can fix dinner, take a shower, or send an email in peace is by plopping them down in front of the TV (a strategy I am not ashamed to admit I use from time to time, i.e., nearly every day). It's what the Iranian regime did during the 2009 protests in an attempt to keep the people from joining the pro-democratic fervor. As the protests gained momentum, the government decided to finally air the *Lord of the Rings* movies on the tightly-controlled national television network.[101] The government had never allowed the films to be shown in Iran before (since they are, after all, about a small group of people who overthrow an oppressive dictator), but in an act of desperation the government risked the films' message in an attempt to distract the people from the protests. Both bread and circuses can keep people too comfortable and dependent on the way things are to bother living differently. Why risk your toys and your entertainment for something as nebulous as justice?

But at the same time, the luxuries and entertainment of our culture can also be used as tools for seeking justice and helping others. During those protests in Iran, the people were able to coordinate and gain the support of the world because of social networking sites like Twitter. While social networking sites are often disdained as a waste of time, accused of replacing real community with fake/virtual community, and derided for turning people into "slacktivists" who think changing their profile picture can change the world, they also can serve as valuable tools to educate and connect people to important causes.

For instance, in Panem, the Capitol controlled the television broadcasts and would only allow people to see what they wanted them to see. The Reapings and the Hunger Games were required viewing since such things kept the districts living in fear. The Capitol also sustained the lie that District 13 had been destroyed by replaying the same outdated shot of a smoldering building. But the rebels were able to tap into that very Capitol-controlled network to spread the truth about the Capitol's lies and injustices. The Capitol had kept the districts disconnected and in ignorance of each other, but the rebels' broadcasts managed to unite the people and move them toward change. The same tool was used for both good and ill.

Many historians argue that the ubiquity of televisions in American households by the 1960s helped bring about the most significant victories of the Civil Rights movement and the widespread acceptance of its aims among white Americans. Unlike today when we have hundreds of television channel options (not to mention DVDs, DVR, and online streaming), during the Civil Rights era there were only three networks on the air, which meant that the majority of the country was all watching more or less the same things at the same time. Thus, when the entire country saw on their nightly news footage of police forces releasing attack dogs and spraying water cannons at non-violent Civil Rights marchers, hearts and minds began to change. Once these images were broadcast to the nation, the brutal realities of racism could no longer be hidden. New technologies put these injustices at the forefront of American communal consciousness and finally generated enough people with civic power willing to say "this is very wrong and needs to stop." The Civil Rights movement succeeded, in part, because its leaders knew how to effectively utilize this new media.

But entertainment and the things we enjoy in life are not only tools to be used for spurring people to action. They can be good in and of themselves. Stories feed our imagination, not only helping us to imagine better worlds, but also granting us joy and wonder. C.S. Lewis described stories as giving us glimpses of the way the world is meant to be, creating joyful pangs of longing in our souls for that world. I was reminded of that when my daughter was 4 years old and watched *The Wizard of Oz* for the first time. At the end of the film she just sat there with tears streaming down her face because she didn't want Dorothy to have to leave the beautiful world of Oz. I have the same reaction every Christmas when, according to our personal tradition, I watch *Love Actually* with my husband. I can't help but get choked up when it gets to the scene toward the end where the little boy whose mom died is running through the airport to tell a girl he loves her because he has learned that if you love someone you have to say it before it is too late. It never fails, my face is covered in tears and I'm grinning ear to ear. That is what stories can do to us. That is why many of my fondest childhood memories revolve around Narnia and *Star Wars*. That is why I gave my kids middle names from characters in *The Lord of the Rings*. That is why I love The Hunger Games. Entertainment is not just a tool or something that drugs us into mindless apathy; it can shape our very imaginations and bring us joy.

So I greatly appreciate that in The Hunger Games books, juxtaposed against the horror of a society numb to the injustice of children being murdered for entertainment, is the reminder that joy and pleasure are also necessary parts of life. If the Capitol is the epitome of bread and circuses placating the masses, District 13 is presented as its direct opposite. In contrast to the outlandish fashions and opulent feasts of the Capitol, in District 13 all the clothing is identical and the tasteless food is distributed according to each person's exact caloric needs. That's why it creates a stir when Finnick and Annie decide to get married in District 13 and the rebel leaders insist that it be a true celebration. Even a small quiet celebration is thrilling to the people in a place where they seem to have no holidays or parties at all. Every child shows up to sing the wedding song, there are more than enough volunteers to make decorations, and the people cannot stop talking about the event. When at the wedding a fiddler strikes up a tune, the refugees of District 12 start dancing, for, as Katniss mentions, "We may have been the smallest, poorest district in Panem, but we know how to dance."[102] Dancing transforms the people whose lives had always been full of hardship, demonstrating that they still have hope and joy.

Similarly, once the rebellion starts weakening the control of the Capitol over the districts, the resources begin to be distributed more evenly among the districts. Instead of the Capitol claiming all the good food for itself and forcing the districts to nearly starve on the poor leftovers, all the districts gain a share in all the resources. After the first shipment of food into District 13, the people there are able to enjoy a stew made with real beef and fresh vegetables. As Katniss enjoys the delicious bounty, she notices that around her in the dining hall, "you can feel the rejuvenating effect that a good meal can bring on. The way it can make people kinder, funnier, more optimistic and remind them it's not a mistake to go on living."[103] They aren't gorging themselves on food while others starve, but neither are they eating tasteless food solely for its energy efficiency. They are enjoying food as it is meant to be enjoyed, where everyone has enough and their own pleasure is not at the expense of someone else's pain. It is an image of what consumption was meant to be.

All too often the tendency of those disgusted by the way in which bread and circuses are used to keep our culture subdued and unwilling to take a stand for justice is to pendulum swing to the opposite side with District 13-like legalism. In this view, if circuses distract us, then all forms of entertainment are to be condemned. If workers in China are mistreated, then we must stop using electronics or buying new clothes entirely. If there are injustices in our food system, then we must only ever eat simple foods. And so forth. But as we see in The Hunger Games, both extremes miss the point.

Enjoying life isn't wrong. Entertainment isn't evil. The Kingdom of God doesn't forbid such things, but they must be done rightly. Entertainment must not consume us to the point that we can't be bothered to care for others. Our enjoyment of life should not justify our exploitation of others. We don't have to give up such things, we simply have to learn to engage them according to the values of the Kingdom of God and not simply the ways of the world. Perhaps the powers that be want us to believe that we must choose between having it all or having nothing. They try to convince us that we must either ignore the plight of others in order to get what we want or else legalistically give it all up. Nothing could be farther from the truth. We see Jesus enjoying life all the time in the Gospels. Perhaps if we didn't only fixate on Jesus's supernatural ability to change water into wine at the wedding of Cana, we would notice the significant point that he cared about people being able to enjoy a celebration. I mean, really enjoy it, with really good wine and lots of it.

Living counter-culturally to the ways of the world does not mean abandoning pleasure and joy—or entertainment and good food for that matter. Not being distracted by bread and circuses does not mean rejecting them entirely; it just means learning to enjoy them the right ways despite pressure and persecution to do otherwise. The blessed in the Kingdom of God know how to live in right relation with others. They do not enjoy what hurts others, but seek for all to share in the joys and blessings of life as God intended. Yes, this may require some to end their over-indulgence or alter their buying habits to support fair practices so that everyone has enough and works under fair conditions. But when people love their neighbors, caring for them in these ways is the least they can do, no matter how the world tries to persuade or persecute them into only caring for themselves.

Just Like I Was Watching the Games

In the summer of 2011 during the unrest and protests in Syria, someone penned a catchy song calling for the president, the symbol of the violent and oppressive government, to leave. A young cement-layer sang the refrain at one of the protests and a few days later his body was pulled out of the river, his throat slashed and his vocal cords ripped out.[104] But this violent attempt to silence the protest only strengthened the voice of the people. His death made the song go viral; young children even sang it in the streets.

That story struck me when I read it because it seemed to have jumped out of the pages of The Hunger Games. During Katniss and Peeta's victory tour of the districts, they encounter thinly-veiled unrest amongst the people. Although Katniss had been threatened to do whatever she could to quiet that unrest, when she gets to District 11 and sees the families of Rue and Thresh, she feels personally compelled to confess how sorry she is for their deaths and that she owes them her life. She thanks the people there for having gathered their meager resources to send her bread in the arena after she sang to Rue and covered her body in flowers. But after Katniss says her unscripted thanks, an old man in the watching crowd starts whistling the tune that Rue used to sing to signal the end of the work day. It is the same tune she and Katniss used to signal safety in the arena. Then in an act that is "too well executed to be spontaneous . . . Every person in the crowd presses the three middle fingers of their left hand against their lips and extends them" to Katniss.[105] It is the District 12 salute, the sign of respect, the last good-bye Katniss gave Rue in the arena, and the people of District 11 in unison offer it to the girl who had defied the Capitol.

Katniss is stunned at their act. As the ceremony ends and she heads back indoors, she realizes that she has left the flowers they gave her on the stage. As she steps back outside to get them she sees Peacekeeping troops dragging the man who had whistled to the top of the steps before the crowd. She then sees them force him to his knees and put a bullet through his head. The audacity of the people in showing allegiance to anything other than the Capitol has harsh repercussions. Voices that speak out about injustice, even if it is just to remember those who lost their lives to the oppressive system, are dangerous to the powers that be. Like the young man in Syria whose vocal cords were ripped out, voices that call for reform or that hold the perpetrators of injustice responsible for their actions are often silenced in extreme ways.

The Capitol in Panem generally keeps dissenters silent through its systems of bread and circuses, but if anyone dares speak out, they permanently silence them by cutting out their tongue. The Avoxes (literally "no voice") not only are incapable of speech, but by law no one is allowed to speak to them either. When she first arrives in the Capitol, Katniss encounters an Avox whom she had seen before. This girl had fled the Capitol and encountered Katniss and Gale while they were out hunting one day, but was soon captured by Capitol forces and turned into an Avox. The memory of that day haunts Katniss and she wants to tell the girl how sorry she is that she didn't do something to help her escape. Katniss reflects, "I'm ashamed I never tried to help her in the woods. That I let the Capitol . . . mutilate her without lifting a finger. Just like I was watching the Games."[106] Katniss remained silent as the Capitol harmed that girl, just like the people in the Capitol remain silent as children die in the Games for their entertainment. In the direct face of injustice, Katniss had placed her own safety before the well-being of this girl, and the girl had suffered the consequences. But after coming face to face with the result of her inaction, Katniss has a hard time living with the fact that she could have done something, but didn't.

The point of persecution is to silence those that call people to a different way. Whether as extreme as destroying a person's physical ability to talk, or censoring their message from the media, or simply mocking them or undermining their message, those in power do what they can to persecute dissenters into silence. When the alternative practices of the communities following Jesus began to disrupt the social and economic systems of Rome, the Romans retaliated harshly. The Christians subverted the tessaere and tribute system by which the Romans controlled the people because they took care of their own poor instead. The Christians also hurt the bottom-line of businesses that made idols and supplies for sacrificing to the gods because they rejected such pagan practices—practices the Romans relied on to create the kind of civic spirit and economic activity that would increase a population's loyalty to Rome and increase tax revenues at the same time.

In Acts 19 we read about how the silversmiths who made idols of Artemis led a riot in protest of the Christians, endangering some of Paul's companions. And in Acts 17 we read of believers being rounded up in Thessalonica and brought before authorities where their accusers claimed, "These people who have been turning the world upside down have come here also . . . They are all acting contrary to the decrees of the emperor" (Acts 17:6-7). Many leaders of the young Christian communities were crucified for turning the world upside-down in this manner, and those who would not swear allegiance to Rome in all aspects of life were frequently thrown into the arena to be eaten by lions. But persecution did not silence them. The Christ-followers met secretly in catacombs and developed secret symbols (like the fish symbol) to communicate with each other. And like the protestors in Iran using Twitter, the early Christians even adopted a new technology called the codex (our modern day book), so they could spread their message though a medium easier to conceal than a bulky scroll.

Only when Christians stopped being persecuted and Christianity became the official religion of Rome under Constantine did its counter-cultural message begin to be silenced. Throughout the ages various groups within Christianity (the Franciscans and the Mennonites are just two examples) have tried to call the Church to once again live in ways other than the greedy and oppressive ways of the world, but such groups are typically either marginalized or themselves coopted and redirected by the mainstream church (some of the more effective methods for silencing dissenting voices). The result is that these days the community of Christ-followers often appears as apologist for the oppressive ways of the world instead of encouraging its members to live in the ways of the Kingdom of God by providing good news to the poor and freedom for the oppressed. Those that choose to affirm the ways of God find persecution just as much from those within the church as from the world, since the two are often indistinguishable.

But, as Katniss discovers, we cannot let fear of persecution or the distractions of life keep us from speaking out in the face of injustice. The memory of the girl who lost her voice because Katniss remained silent haunts Katniss, leading her to use what voice she has as the Mockingjay—the symbol of the rebellion—for the sake of others. Similarly, there are many in our world today who have no voice except ours. If we stay safe and distracted and accept the status quo, their suffering will continue.

If we are willing to use our voices, then we need to tell companies like Apple (with our voice and our money) that we care more for workers in China than getting the latest iPhone or gadget. We need to tell chocolate companies that we do not support child slavery. We don't abandon joy or pleasure, but we don't stay silent and force others to sacrifice themselves for us either. We must use our voices to defend the dignity of people from different races, ethnic groups, or genders when we hear them being demeaned or see them being silenced. We must speak up about atrocities and unfair practices in both the past and the present so as to hold the perpetrators responsible for their actions. We must stand with those the world exploits, treats as disposable, or uses as mere objects, and claim them as our brothers and sisters, fearfully and wonderfully made in the image of God. It won't be popular, for bullies don't like being told to stop picking on the weak. They will turn on us and try to make us be quiet, even try to use the name of Jesus to silence our voices.

But, as Jesus said, it is far more blessed to face persecution for living in the ways of the Kingdom of God, than to abandon the needy for the siren call of the bread and circuses of the world.

Conclusion
Dandelions in the Spring

"You are the light of the world. A city built on a hill cannot be hid. No one after lighting a lamp puts it under the bushel basket, but on the lampstand, and it gives light to all in the house. In the same way, let your light shine before others, so that they may see your good works and give glory to your Father in heaven."
~ Matthew 5:14-16

There is no happily-ever-after at the end of The Hunger Games series. There is hope and some joy, but no fairy tale ending. The rebellion doesn't make the world perfect. The dystopia of Panem does not suddenly morph into a utopian paradise free of corruption where no one hungers and oppression and injustice have disappeared. Those that died in the war and in the Hunger Games are still dead. The vast inequalities of the land will take years to balance out, if the people can commit to the process for that long. The masterminds behind the rebellion have moved on to the next thing to entertain the masses—a televised singing competition. And the hero of the story, Katniss Everdeen, the girl who was on fire, is left broken.

Throughout the books Katniss struggles with her identity. The world had demanded that she be so many different people that she has difficulty accepting who she truly is. The young girl had to become the provider for her family after her father died. As tribute in the Hunger Games they try to get her to adopt a more appealing persona, but as Katniss confesses, "At once it's clear I cannot gush. We try me playing cocky, but I just don't have the arrogance. Apparently, I'm too vulnerable for ferocity, I'm not witty. Funny. Sexy. Or mysterious."[107] But she has spirit; she knows how to fight to survive. Becoming the girl on fire helps her survive the Games and commit to helping others afterward. Yet even that must be hidden as the Capitol finds it too dangerous and tries to instead present her as a silly girl in love. During the process Katniss reflects, "I feel like dough, being kneaded and reshaped again and again."[108] She eventually realizes that she must fight for what is right, but even that part of her gets appropriated by the rebellion as they turn the Mockingjay into their mascot. She becomes their soldier until she can take the hypocrisy no more. She wants to use her voice to help create a better world for all, but as she admits, "Gradually, I am forced to accept who I am. A badly burned girl with no wings. With no fire. And no sister."[109]

At the end of the tale, she is sent home alone and broken. No one knows what to do with her once the war is over. Katniss succumbs to depression and despair, barely living at all in the wake of all that has happened. Only slowly and tentatively does she find the ability to mourn what she has lost and the courage to start piecing her life back together. When Peeta, still dealing with his own demons, returns home as well, they discover together how to move past the ways they were used and have faith in hope again. Katniss discovers that what she needs to survive is not a fire kindled with rage and hatred, but "the dandelion in the spring. The bright yellow flower that means rebirth instead of destruction. The promise that life can go on, no matter how bad our losses. That it can be good again."[110] She finds that in love. And it is in her loving and supportive relationship with Peeta that they together work to rebuild the world. The nightmares don't ever go away. And they know they will have to tell their children the truth of the horrors they lived through to help them have courage and hope as well. But they survive. As Katniss says, years after the end of the war on the days when enjoying life seems impossible, "That's when I make a list in my head of every act of goodness I've seen someone do. It's like a game. Repetitive. Even a little tedious after more than twenty years. But there are much worse games to play."[111]

Sometimes it's hard to remember the good. In a world full of injustice, pain, oppression, and persecution it can be hard to find joy and continue to have hope that the dreams of God can be realized. Like Katniss, we must remind ourselves of where we have experienced those moments that affirm life. I find that stories like The Hunger Games provide me with some of those moments of hope. They remind me that although I will constantly stumble amidst hardship, and that I will never bring about a perfect world through my efforts alone, it is still worthwhile to hunger and thirst after righteousness. That however dismal the outlook may appear, it is still blessed to live in the ways of God's Kingdom. That Katniss struggles and suffers and has to remind herself to remember the good helps me know that I am not alone. As Sam said to Frodo in the film version of *The Lord of the Rings*, these stories mean something because they remind us to hold on to the truth that "there's some good in the world . . . and it's worth fighting for."[112]

And so I pray for God's Kingdom to come on earth as it is in heaven even as I live into its blessed ways in the present. As theologian Jürgen Moltmann wrote, "Those who hope in Christ can no longer put up with reality as it is, but begin to suffer under it, to contradict it. Peace with God means conflict with the world, for the goad of the promised future stabs inexorably into the flesh of every unfulfilled present."[113] That hope in the way of love that transforms the world gives me courage to live in its ways. I don't want to hide my light out of fear of persecution or of losing the bread and circuses I hold dear, but instead I want to let it shine into the dark places of injustice and oppression, illuminating hope. And to do that I must embody the call to love.

Katniss's father had once told her when they were out foraging in the woods and came upon the blue tubers of the katniss plant for which she was named, "As long as you can find yourself, you'll never starve."[114] In that world where to be hungry meant one was at the mercy of the Capitol and therefore had no hope, finding herself and discovering her identity apart from the controlling ways of others held the key to her survival. From the moments when she covered Rue with flowers and defied the Capitol with the berries at the end of the Games, she knew that having the courage to stand on the side of love against the injustices of the world was part of who she is. And though she took a few detours in getting there, Katniss finally realizes that the trust and joy that love affirms are the building blocks to a better world. It is difficult, and love always involves the risk of suffering, but like the dandelion ushering in the spring, it is where one finds hope.

As You Read: Questions for Discussion and Reflection

Introduction
Let the Games Begin

1. Before you start: Think of important moments for you in the Hunger Games. Why and how did they affect you?
2. Clawson says "stories have always been the best way to pose challenging questions about the world around us." What questions does the Hunger Games series pose?
3. In what ways can popular fiction like The Hunger Games series serve to illuminate the Gospel and provide readers with spiritual/theological insights?
4. Clawson uses the world of Panem to comment on our own world throughout this book. What do you find to be the most striking similarities between the two worlds?
5. Clawson compares living in the ways of the Kingdom of God with working to help God's dreams be realized on earth as in heaven. From your knowledge of the Bible, how would you describe God's dreams for our world?

Chapter One
The Poor in Spirit: Living in the United States of Panem

1. Before you start: "Blessed are the poor in spirit, for theirs is the kingdom of heaven" (Matthew 5:3). Reflect on this beatitude and the ways it could relate to The Hunger Games.
2. The ways the Capitol stays in control of the districts are clear – hunger, violence, and the games. Where are similar systems of oppression at work in our own world?
3. From one point of view, Capitol citizens are despicably selfish. One can make the argument, however, that they are simply ignorant of the effects of their actions. What do

you think? Is ignorance a valid excuse for remaining complicit in oppression?

4. The Roman Empire of Jesus' time and the Capitol in the world of The Hunger Games used "bread and circuses" to distract the masses from caring about the oppressed or working for justice. What are the distractions in our world that keep us from responsibly working for a better world?

5. Clawson shows how Jesus and Katniss both live counter-culturally, but they were both part of the oppressed lower classes that were often necessarily at odds with the dominant culture already. How does Clawson suggest those in the middle and upper classes (i.e. participants in the dominant culture) can also live counter-culturally today?

Chapter Two
Those Who Mourn: Remembering the Things It Would Be a Crime to Forget

1. Before you start: "Blessed are those who mourn, for they will be comforted" (Matthew 5:4). Reflect on this beatitude and the ways it could relate to The Hunger Games.

2. One of the most common criticisms of The Hunger Games is its depictions of extreme violence. Clawson makes the argument that remembering (and depicting) violence and the harm it inflicts is necessary for true mourning. Do you agree or disagree? What are the benefits and dangers of telling stories of the true cost of violence (both fictional and historical)?

3. How does preventing the oppressed from mourning sustain the Capitol's and Rome's power? How is mourning prevented in our own world? Why?

4. Clawson focuses on the power of mourning as a healing force. Has this worked in your life? Where could it be used in our world?

5. Clawson writes of the need to recognize communal sins. What are some of the communal sins that you see in our world? Why does our society often seem to struggle to even acknowledge the reality of communal sin?

Chapter Three
The Meek: Supporting One Body, Many Districts

1. Before you start: "Blessed are the meek, for they will inherit the earth" (Matthew 5:5). Reflect on this beatitude and the ways it could relate to The Hunger Games.
2. "Living meekly is vastly different than simply letting others walk all over you." What does meekness mean in your life?
3. If meekness is one of the ways of the Kingdom of God, are Panem's district citizens right to rise up violently? Is there ever a point when meekness is no longer the ethical option?
4. Is the Stoic version or Paul's version of the body metaphor more prevalent in our world? What are the challenges to living in ways that care for the entire body instead of just your small part?
5. Clawson argues that the violence in The Hunger Games helps to teach of the evils of war and oppression. While this may be true, many still believe the books are too graphic for young teens. Is the exposure worth the lesson? What lesson does it teach?

Chapter Four
Those Who Hunger and Thirst for Righteousness: Loving Like the Boy with the Bread

1. Before you start: "Blessed are those who hunger and thirst for righteousness, for they will be filled" (Matthew 5:6). Reflect on this beatitude and the ways it could relate to The Hunger Games.

2. Clawson immediately draws a line between satiable, righteous hunger and insatiable hunger. What are the things the world encourages us to hunger after that distract us from hungering after the ways of the Kingdom of God? What is the price of hungering after unfulfilling things?

3. In the Bible the terms righteousness and justice are synonymous. What distinctions are there between the two words in the ways we commonly use them today? Why do you think they've become separated like that? What would it look like to hunger and thirst after justice?

4. Peeta repeatedly demonstrates love and concern for others even when it requires sacrifice on his part. What sacrifices might be required of you in order to live righteously/justly?

5. Clawson is concerned that the church often focuses on personal purity over the well-being (shalom) of the community. If both are important, how does one balance the two? Where is the line between righteous and self-righteous?

Chapter Five
The Merciful: Recognizing the Humanity of Others

1. Before you start: "Blessed are the merciful, for they will receive mercy" (Matthew 5:7). Reflect on this beatitude and the ways it could relate to The Hunger Games.

2. In what ways does our culture encourage vengeance and retribution (e.g. popular entertainment, media, political rhetoric, religious messages, etc.)? Are there any cultural factors that encourage mercy?

3. At one point Gale suggests to Katniss that killing people is no different than killing animals. How does dehumanizing others make it easier to harm them? In what ways do you see this being done in our world?

4. How does the act of mercy that God extends to us through Jesus encourage us to similarly offer mercy to others?

What difficulties do you face in offering respect, love, and forgiveness to those different than yourself?

5. Clawson points out that entering into relationships with the would-be despised helps them to see you as human as well. Can you think of times this has happened in your life?

Chapter Six
The Pure in Heart: Looking Past Artificial Exteriors

1. Before you start: "Blessed are the pure in heart, for they will see God" (Matthew 5:8). Reflect on this beatitude and the ways it could relate to The Hunger Games.

2. Clawson argues that the pure in heart are those that see where God is at work in the world and commit themselves to that work. What might being purely devoted to the ways of the Kingdom of God look like in your life?

3. Jesus accused the Pharisees of being whitewashed tombs, beautiful on the outside but full of decay on the inside. In The Hunger Games the outward luxury of the Capitol hides the greed and selfishness within. Where do you see beautiful exteriors masking impurity within?

4. Katniss initially dislikes Haymitch and Finnick, but after she learns their stories she understands how their actions stem from pure hearts. When has learning someone's story helped you understand and sympathize with them better?

5. Clawson argues that Katniss had to resist the Capitol's laws in order to do the right thing. What do you think about this? When might breaking a rule actually be the right thing to do?

Chapter Seven
The Peacemakers: Subverting the Games of Violence

1. Before you start: "Blessed are the peacemakers, for they will be called children of God" (Matthew 5:9). Reflect on this beatitude and the ways it could relate to The Hunger Games.

2. Katniss refers to the refusal of District 12 to applaud her volunteering for the Reaping as the boldest form of dissent they can manage. How could such a refusal be seen as an act of peacemaking? What in our own world should we refuse to applaud even when others do?

3. Clawson argues that games of revenge are ultimately futile since responding to oppression with violence often simply leads to more violence and more oppression. Where have you found this to be true?

4. Jesus encouraged his followers to respond to oppression with acts of creative peacemaking. What is meant by "creative peacemaking" and how is it an alternative to either violent response or passive acceptance of oppression?

5. After the rebellion when President Coin suggested holding another Hunger Games to punish Capitol leaders, Katniss reflects, "Nothing has changed. Nothing ever changes." What do you think? Is change possible?

Chapter Eight
The Persecuted: Finding One's Voice in a Distracted World

1. Before you start: "Blessed are those who are persecuted for righteousness' sake, for theirs is the kingdom of heaven" (Matthew 5:10). Reflect on this beatitude and the ways it could relate to The Hunger Games.

2. Clawson argues that people often get so attached to luxuries and entertainments that they assume they are being persecuted when they are called to live sacrificially instead. Where have you seen this happening?

3. When Katniss stands up to the injustices of the Capitol, she faces persecution. Jesus promised that living in ways that promote justice will lead to persecution. Have you experienced persecution for following the way of Jesus by standing up for justice? How?
4. Clawson suggests that entertainment and enjoying life are not inherently bad, but they must be done rightly, in ways that do not harm others. What might it look like to enjoy life rightly?
5. Katniss later feels ashamed for having remained silent as the Capitol captured a girl and turned her into an Avox. She compares it to watching the Games – passively watching while others were harmed. Where in our culture do we frequently remain silent as others face injustice and oppression?

Conclusion
Dandelions in the Spring

1. Before you start: Reflect on the ending of The Hunger Games series. Did you find it to be hopeful, disturbing, or both? Why?
2. Katniss ultimately discovers that she needs not the fires of rage and revenge, but the hopefulness of love that encourages new life. Do you agree that love always provides more hope than revenge? Why? Is it possible to embrace both, or are they mutually exclusive?
3. Clawson argues that just as Katniss had to discover her identity apart from the ways of the world, so too Christians must resist the ways of the world in order to live in the ways of the Kingdom of God. What might this look like in your own life?
4. Stories like The Hunger Games can serve as reminders that there is good in the world that is worth fighting for. Where do you see good in this world? What will you now do to fight for it?

Recommended for Further Reading

Walter Brueggemann, *Out of Babylon*, Abingdon, 2010.

Julie Clawson, *Everyday Justice: The Global Impact of Our Daily Choices,* InterVarsity Press, 2009.

Richard A. Horsley, *Jesus and Empire: The Kingdom of God and the New World Disorder*, Fortress Press, 2002.

Wes Howard-Brook, *Come Out My People!: God's Call Out of Empire in the Bible and Beyond*, Orbis Books, 2010.

Brian McLaren, *Everything Must Change: When the World's Biggest Problems and Jesus' Good News Collide*, Thomas Nelson, 2009.

Joerg Rieger, *Christ & Empire: From Paul to Postcolonial Times*, Augsburg Fortress, 2007.

Desmond Tutu, *No Future Without Forgiveness*, Image, 2000.

Brian Walsh and Sylvia Keesmaat, *Colossians Remixed: Subverting the Empire*, InterVarsity Press, 2004.

About the Author

Julie Clawson is the author of *Everyday Justice: The Global Impact of Our Daily Choices* and a frequent speaker on the topics of Christianity, culture, and justice. She holds degrees in English and History and a Master's degree in Intercultural Studies from Wheaton College, and is currently studying theology at the Seminary of the Southwest. Julie is a complete sci-fi/fantasy geek who enjoys exploring the ways great stories like The Hunger Games can help Christians understand their faith. She also just loves really good stories. Julie lives in Austin, Texas with her husband Mike and two imaginative children Emmaline Eowyn and Aidan Elessar. She can be found writing about faith, justice, culture, and whatever else interests her at www.julieclawson.com.

Endnotes

[1] Claire Bradford and Kerry Mallan, *New World Orders in Contemporary Children's Literature* (New York: Palgrave Macmillan, 2008), 29.

[2] Ibid., 2.

[3] I understand how problematic the term "Kingdom of God" is for some. That language of a King can connote a domineering patriarchy and has ties to oppressive colonial regimes—both of which work against the hopeful life-affirming reality that it is meant to convey. For that reason, some have suggested that better translations of the term might be "Realm of God," "Kinship of God," or "Dreams of God." While all those terms convey what is at the core of the term, none of them have yet gained widespread use. At the same time "Kingdom of God" theology that speaks to many of the themes in this book is gaining influence in the church. So even as I acknowledge the tensions related to the term, I have chosen to use the more common term "Kingdom of God" in this book.

[4] Brian McLaren, *Everything Must Change: Jesus, Global Crises, and a Revolution of Hope* (Nashville: Thomas Nelson, 2007), 114.

[5] Suzanne Collins, *The Hunger Games* (New York: Scholastic Press, 2008), 6

[6] See N.T. Wright, *The New Testament and the People of God* (1992) and Richard Horsley (Ed.) *In the Shadow of Empire* (2008).

[7] Collins, *The Hunger Games*, 65.

[8] Richard Horsley, *Jesus and Empire: The Kingdom of God and the New World Disorder* (Minneapolis: Fortress Press, 2003), 29.

[9] Collins, *The Hunger Games*, 6.

[10] Ibid., 19.

[11] "Some 200 Women gang-raped Near Congo UN Base," *Times Live*, August 24, 2010, <http://www.timeslive.co.za/africa/article619495.ece/Some-200-women-gang-raped-near-Congo-UN-base>

[12] "2007 Uprising in Burma," Burma Campaign UK, <http://www.burmacampaign.org.uk/index.php/burma/about-burma/about-burma/2007-uprising-in-burma>

[13] "Cut the Strings," Jubilee USA, <http://www.jubileeusa.org/truth-about-debt/cut-the-strings.html>

[14] For more details on how people around the world pay for our consumption see my book *Everyday Justice: The Global Impact of Our Daily Choices* (2009).

[15] Suzanne Collins, *Catching Fire* (New York: Scholastic Press, 2009), 175-176.

[16] Suzanne Collins, *Mockingjay* (New York: Scholastic Press, 2010), 169.

[17] Walter Wink, *Jesus and Nonviolence: A Third Way* (Minneapolis: Fortress Press, 2003), 14.

[18] Pliny, "Letters, 10.96-97," < http://www9.georgetown.edu/faculty/jod/texts/pliny.html>.

[19] Barbara Brown Taylor, *Speaking of Sin: The Lost Language of Salvation* (Lanham, MD: Cowley Publications, 2000), 46.

[20] Collins, *The Hunger Games*, 308.

[21] Martin Hengel, *Crucifixion* (Minneapolis: Augsburg Fortress Press, 1977), 50.

[22] Ashley Fantz, "Fallen pilot's 10-year-old: Don't forget my dad," August 11, 2011, < http://articles.cnn.com/2011-08-09/us/chinook.son.ireport_1_dad-chinook-father?_s=PM:US>.

[23] Esther Yue Ng, "Mirror Reading and Guardians of Women in the Early Roman Empire," *Journal of Theological Studies*, 59.2 (2008), 685-686.

[24] Collins, *Mockingjay*, 387.

[25] Collins, *Catching Fire*, 240.

[26] Amanda Paulson, "Texas Textbook War," May 19, 2010, <http://www.csmonitor.com/USA/Education/2010/0519/Texas-textbook-war-Slavery-or-Atlantic-triangular-trade>.

[27] "Merkel 'bows with shame' before Holocaust victims," March 19, 2008, < http://www.abc.net.au/news/2008-03-19/merkel-bows-with-shame-before-holocaust-victims/1077210>.

[28] Nicholas Kulish, "Germany Confronts Holocaust Legacy Anew," January 29, 2008, <http://www.nytimes.com/2008/01/29/world/europe/29nazi.html?pagewanted=all>.

[29] James Loewen, *Lies My Teacher Told Me* (New York: Touchstone, 2007), 91-92.

[30] Richard Twiss, *One Church, Many Tribes: Following Jesus the Way God Made You,* (Regal Books: Venture, CA., 2000), 67.

[31] Walter Brueggemann, *Out of Babylon* (Nashville: Abingdon, 2010), 35.

[32] See Desmond Tutu's *No Future Without Forgiveness* (New York: Image, 2000).

[33] Soong-Chan Rah, *The Next Evangelicalism: Freeing the Church from Western Cultural Captivity* (InterVarsity Press: Downers Grove, IL., 2009), 41.

[34] Collins, *The Hunger Games,* 234.

[35] Ibid., 22.

[36] Brian Walsh and Sylvia Keesmaat, *Colossians Remixed* (Downers Grove, IL: InterVarsity Press, 2004), 175.

[37] Tutu, 93.

[38] Michelle V. Lee, *Paul, the Stoics, and the Body of Christ* (Cambridge: Cambridge University Press, 2006), 10.

[39] Collins, *Catching Fire*, 23.

[40] See <http://www.drhorrible.com/>.

[41] Collins, *Catching Fire,* 123.

[42] Wes Howard-Brook, *Come Out My People!: God's Call Out of Empire and Beyond* (Maryknoll, NY: Orbis, 2010), 428.

[43] Ibid., 428.

[44] Collins, *Mockingjay*, 150.

[45] Jeffrey McMurrey, "Vacation Liberty School," Huffington Post, July 15, 2010, <http://www.huffingtonpost.com/2010/07/15/vacation-liberty-school-t_n_647822.html>.

[46] "Frequently challenged books of the 21st century," American Library Association, <http://www.ala.org/advocacy/banned/frequentlychallenged/21stcenturychallenged#2010>

[47] Collins, *Mockingjay*, 239.

[48] Ibid., 91.

[49] Collins, *Catching Fire*, 232.

[50] Collins, *The Hunger Games*, 26.

[51] Ibid., 141.

[52] Dorothy Day, *Loaves and Fishes* (Maryknoll, NY: Orbis, 2007), 215.

[53] Larry L. Rasmussen, *Dietrich Bonhoeffer: Reality and Resistance* (Louisville, KY: Westminster John Knox, 2005), 51-52.

[54] Collins, *The Hunger Games*, 32.

[55] Collins, Mockingjay, 23.

[56] Rita Nakashima Brock and Gabriella Lettini, "How Do We Repair the Souls of Those Returning from Iraq?," *Huffington Post Religion*, October 26, 2011, http://www.huffingtonpost.com/rita-nakashima-brock-ph-d/the-war-is-coming-home-so_b_1027499.html.

[57] Brett T. Litz, Nathan Stein, Eileen Delaney, Leslie Lebowitz, William P. Nash, Caroline Silva, and Shira Maguen, "Moral injury and moral repair in war veterans: A preliminary model and intervention strategy," *Clinical Psychology Review* 29:8 (2009), doi:10.1016/j.cpr.2009.07.003.

[58] Eli Clifton, "Suicide Rates Surged Among Veterans," *Inter Press Service*, January 13, 2010, http://ipsnews.net/news.asp?idnews=49971.

[59] Purchasing items that are Fair Trade certified or sweatshop-free are easy ways to pay a fair price for the things we consume.

[60] Collins, *Mockingjay*, 243.

[61] Ibid., 214.

[62] Collins, *The Hunger Games,* 288.

[63] See John 8.

[64] Luke 15

[65] Collins, *The Hunger Games,* 40.

[66] Ibid.

[67] Ibid., 243.

[68] Alfie Kohn, *Unconditional Parenting* (New York: Atria Books, 2005), 101-102.

[69] Gwynne Dyer, *War: The Lethal Custom* (New York: Carroll and Graf Publishers, 2004), 54-57.

[70] Gwynne Dyer, "Post Traumatic Psycho Babble," April 27, 2011, http://gwynnedyer.com/2011/post-traumatic-psycho-babble/

[71] Collins, *Mockingjay*, 53.

[72] Ibid.

[73] Ibid., 257.

[74] Collins, *The Hunger Games,* 59.

[75] Collins, *Catching Fire*, 209.

[76] Collins, *Mockingjay,* 170.

[77] Collins, *Catching Fire,* 75.

[78] Martin Luther King Jr., "Letter from a Birmingham Jail," <http://www.africa.upenn.edu/Articles_Gen/Letter_Birmingha m.html>.

[79] Collins, *The Hunger Games,* 211.

[80] Collins, *Mockingjay*, 370.

[81] Ibid., 214-215.

[82] Howard-Brook, 414.

[83] Walter Wink, *Jesus and Nonviolence: A Third Way* (Minneapolis: Fortress Press, 2003), 70.

[84] Collins, *Mockingjay*, 377.

[85] Wink, 14-26.

[86] Ibid., 21.

[87] Collins, *The Hunger Games,* 22-23.

[88] Collins, *Catching Fire*, 258.

[89] Jim Wallis, *God's Politics* (New York: HarperCollins, 2005), 106.

[90] For more information see <http://en.wikipedia.org/wiki/ Women_of_Liberia_Mass_Action_for_Peace>.

[91] I highly recommend the documentary *Pray the Devil Back to Hell* (2008), which tells the story of the Liberian women's peace movement.

[92] Annysa Johnson, "Churches skirt shelter regulations," *JSOnline*, Dec. 14, 2010, < http://www.jsonline.com/features/religion/111894444.html>

[93] For more information see <http://en.wikipedia.org/wiki/Bhopal_disaster>.

[94] Interesting choice of name. Jude is the saint of lost causes, and 'finisterra" mean the ends of the earth.

[95] Watch the broadcast at <http://www.youtube.com/watch?v=LiWlvBro9eI>.

[96] Collins, *The Hunger Games,* 356-357.

[97] Nicholas Wolterstorff, *Justice: Rights and Wrongs* (Princeton: NJ: Princeton University Press, 2008), 111.

[98] Collins, *The Hunger Games,* 357-358.

[99] "Jesus is a Liberal Democrat," *The Colbert Report*, December 16, 2010, < http://www.colbertnation.com/the-colbert-report-videos/368914/december-16-2010/jesus-is-a-liberal-democrat>.

[100] Charles Duhigg and David Barboza, "In China, Human Costs Are Built Into an iPad," *The New York Times*, January 25, 2012, <http://www.nytimes.com/2012/01/26/business/ieconomy-apples-ipad-and-the-human-costs-for-workers-in-china.html?_r=1&hp=&pagewanted=all>

[101] "Watching *The Lord of the Rings* in Tehran," *Time World*, June 25, 2009, <http://www.time.com/time/world/article/0,8599,1906740,00.html>

[102] Collins, *Mockingjay*, 226.

[103] Ibid., 241.

[104] Anthony Shadid, "Lyrical Message for Syrian Leader," *The New York Times*, July 21, 2011, <http://www.nytimes.com/2011/07/22/world/middleeast/22poet.html?_r=3>

[105] Collins, *Catching Fire*, 61.

[106] Collins, *The Hunger Games*, 85.

[107] Ibid., 118.

[108] Collins, *Catching Fire*, 166.

[109] Collins, *Mockingjay*, 350.

[110] Ibid., 388

[111] Ibid., 390.

[112] *The Lord of the Rings: The Two Towers*, Directed by Peter Jackson (2002: New Line Cinema).

[113] Jürgen Moltmann, *Theology of Hope*, trans. James W. Leitch (New York: SCM Press Ltd., 1967), 21.

[114] Collins, *The Hunger Games*, 52.

CPSIA information can be obtained at www.ICGtesting.com
Printed in the USA
LVOW01s0609100814

398396LV00018B/661/P